motocross
2004 Grand Prix Review

motocross
2004 Grand Prix Review

Adam Wheeler

TEMPUS

First published 2005

Tempus Publishing Ltd
The Mill, Brimscombe Port
Stroud, Gloucestershire gl5 2qg
www.tempus-publishing.com

British Library Cataloguing in Publication Data.
A catalogue record for this book is available from the British Library.

0 7524 3413 6

Designed and typeset by Chris May – www.solographik.co.uk
Origination by Tempus Publishing.
Printed and bound in Great Britain.

Ben Townley
MX2 world champion

W hat is the secret to riding a bike fast? I have been asked that question so many times, but the truth is that there is no secret. I was put on this earth for one reason. My heart beats for MX; it is my passion. I've been involved in the sport for fourteen years now and for as long as I can remember, my life, and that of my family, has revolved around motocross. On 11 September 2004 my mechanic held up the pit board saying 'Your dream has come true'. Everything in my fourteen years of racing passed through my head; both highs and lows as I completed my last few corners before crossing the finish line as the new 2004 MX2 World Champion.

Motocross right now is still developing its professionalism. On the inside it's the same sport it always was and will always be: 'ordinary people doing extraordinary things'. We can always ask if it is heading in the right direction. Personally I think change is great, I love it. You can't leave your foot on second base if you want to get to third. I have only been in the GPs for four years and in my eyes it is moving forward in a positive way. This book is a good example. Every great sport has an 'annual'. It is a big honour for me to introduce the Motocross World Championship class of 2004. The images and memories caught within these pages will act as time capsule for what was a fantastic season. Everyone has heroes, mentors and people they look up to, whether they admit it or not. 2005 and MX1 brings a huge challenge for me. I not only admire those people, but I'll be at the start gate with them. I will be in Belgium at the beginning of April with the same chance of glory, if not more, than anyone else on the line.

I've always possessed a love for racing bikes and approached every race with enthusiasm and determination to give it my best. That will never change.

Enjoy the trip through 2004.

'BT'

2004 FIM Motocross World Championships:
The gate drops on a new era

The World Championships were a fountain for young talent like Townley, Rattray, Strijbos, Leok, Cairoli and Pourcel.

For 2004 the FIM World Championship had arrived at its third incarnation in four years. Motocross was weary of change and desperately needed a set of 'stabilisers' so that it could set off in the right direction with momentum. After entertaining three classes with one race each in 2001 and 2002 (125, 250 and 500cc) the acknowledgement of the growing influence and commercial popularity of modern 4-stroke technology led to the formulation of 125, MXGP and 650 classifications in 2003. The premier MXGP competition, comprising of 250cc 2-stroke machines and 450cc 4-stroke motorcycles, was won by Stefan Everts, still using a one-race system.

The fifth season of the new millennium swept in further enhancements. Grand Prix motocross transformed again and for the immediate future has settled on 'MX1' and 'MX2' (essentially the MXGP and old 125cc categories) but reverting back to the time-honoured two moto format, providing four races in one day. The oldest of the classes, the 500cc – the first World Championship to be permanently established back in 1957 – had since become '650', was finally reduced to 'MX3' and run as a separate support series along with the 125cc European Championship. While MX1 was pushed as the elite category with a new privileged-entry list, MX2 (a mixture of 125cc 2-strokes and 250cc 4-strokes) was seen as the junior supply line to the slightly more revered class in terms of publicity and TV attention. The readoption of the two moto programme was hailed by fans of the sport worldwide, as motocross stopped bending to the demands and aesthetic of modern live television and returned to tradition.

Youthstream were the new promoters and their president, Giuseppe Luongo, who controlled the sport as part of the Action Group firm until 2001, seemed to be ploughing firmly ahead with his (and the FIM's) vision of how GP racing could tackle the future. He cited wide media exposure, enticement of young riders to stay this side of the Atlantic, a large sixteen-race international calendar, decent television coverage and moulding what essentially is a more open and grass-roots sport into a professional and marketable entity. Some good ideas such as the promotion of the 125cc European Championship as a pathway to Grand Prix have begun to take off, but the means by which Youthstream wished to install of all these factors proved not to be so popular. Prize-money cuts and charges for the teams, while demanding that they portray a better marketable image and pay for the extra travelling with a larger calendar, became sore points. The riders were disgruntled by the financial devaluation of their efforts and the

Grand Prix benefited from modern circuits like Arreton on the Isle of Wight and was bolstered by equally efficient TV coverage in 2004.

teams felt harshly done by. 2004 became a term of consternation in a Grand Prix paddock where the minority had little opportunity to voice their opinion and be taken seriously. Political activities were always close to the racing, with riders' meetings, strikes and the formulation of MXTAG (Motocross Team Advisory Group) to air the teams' grievances, all arising in the seven-month sixteen-race championship.

Off-track adversity aside, the overall feeling about the 2004 season was a good one. MX1 and MX2 worked excellently with some captivating racing and more value for money for the spectator, in turn increasing attendances at the circuits and letting more venues consider running a motocross Grand Prix without incurring a cash loss. For their first attempt Youthstream delivered a decent calendar that sadly was top heavy with Benelux races but also boasted some memorable and atmospheric events such as Namur, South Africa, the British

Grand Prix, the Italian round and the Motocross of Nations. The presentation of the series was mostly impressive, with a larger paddock, and the facilities were generally up to scratch. The Youthstream press releases at the end of the year stated that motocross had reached more people than ever before thanks to the television and media.

Stefan Everts was again the best MX1 rider and cemented his legendary status further with another display of superlative motocross, even though he faced his toughest competition in years from the likes of Mickael Pichon, Cedric Melotte, Brian Jorgensen, Kevin Strijbos, Josh Coppins and Steve Ramon. The MX1 class had five different winners in sixteen events and seven different moto victors from a possible thirty-two races. Ben Townley clinched his first World Championship in the MX2 series that showcased some exciting young talent for the future as well as some new 4-stroke machinery. Often more chaotic and frantic than the

Above: Josh Coppins tests the limit of the Bridgestone tyres riding the Honda CRF 450R.
Opposite Page: Yoshitaka Atsuta loses grip in a swarm of mud as the new MX1 class comes alive.

senior class, MX2 was also far less predictable. Eight different riders won MX2 motos while six scored Grand Prix winners' trophies, three for the first time. The 2004 campaign was, for many riders, one of the longest. It invited career-defining moments of glory, disaster, misfortune, high drama and injury. This is the story.

Motocross is such an intense sport both physically and mentally. It is also one of the most photogenic in the world and a great reason why this book has come to exist. Enjoy the trip.

The 'Lines'

MX1:

Honda: Mickael Pichon, Brian Jorgensen, Josh Coppins, Gordon Crockard, Yoshitaka Atsuta.
Yamaha: Stefan Everts, Cedric Melotte.
Suzuki: Joel Smets, Kevin Strijbos.
Aprilia: Javier Garcia Vico, Thomas Traversini.
KTM: Kenneth Gundersen, Steve Ramon.
TM: Enrico Oddenino, Antti Pyrhonen.

MX2:

KTM: Ben Townley, Marc de Reuver, Tyla Rattray.
Yamaha: Alessio Chiodi, Andrea Bartolini, Claudio Federici, Antonio Cairoli, Andrew McFarlane, Patrick Caps.
Honda: Jussi Vehvilainen, Jamie Dobb, Carl Nunn, Jeff Dement.
Kawasaki: Stephen Sword, Mickael Maschio, Sebastien Pourcel.

Supporting cast:

Tanel Leok (**Suzuki**), Ken de Dijcker (**Honda**), James Noble (**Honda**), Billy Mackenzie (**Yamaha**), Luigi Seguy (**Yamaha**).

Supporting cast:

Aigar Leok (**KTM**), Gareth Swanepoel (**KTM**), Akira Narita (**Honda**).

Top Ten Riders
2004

1. Stefan Everts (Belgium)

Yamaha L&M Motocross Team

GP wins: 7

Moto wins: 13

Podiums: 14

World Championship pos: 1st (MX1)

Titles: 8, MX1, MXGP (2003), 500cc
(2002, 2001), 250cc (1997, 96, 95),
125cc (1991)

At the end of 2003 Stefan Everts claimed the MXGP title, recorded a historic
clean sweep of the final Grand Prix of the season at Ernee in France (125, MXGP
and 650 motos all on the same day) and also won every 125 race in the second
half of the season. After helping Belgium to victory in the Motocross of Nations he
then packed his bags and captured the prestigious ISDE enduro title. In 2004 he
reigned supreme for his eighth crown, missing the podium only twice in sixteen
Grand Prix and took more Nations acclaim.

Everts is the most talented off-road racer ever. He is also courteous, open and
immensely professional; the ultimate combination of natural talent, dedication
and application. Stefan is consistency personified and this explains his success
rate and immeasurable impact on the sport. He rarely makes mistakes and never
fades. The thirty-one-year-old is fast from the first moment of the opening race to
the last minute of the final moto and it is up to the others to catch him. Then of
course there is that wonderful flowing style...

2. Mickael Pichon (France)

Tiscali Martin Honda

GP wins: 6

Moto wins: 10

Podiums: 10

World Championship pos: 2nd (MX1)

Titles: 2, 250cc (2002, 2001)

Mickael Pichon was the only real threat to Stefan Everts. It was the first year
for Mickael on a 4-stroke and he was also making a comeback from the knee
ligament injury that kept him off the bike for five months. This could explain his
slightly unsteady start to the season but the crash at Teutschenthal in round five
was a result of Pichon's tendency to push too much while already riding on the
edge. The results that day and the after-effects in terms of recovering from the
spill lost him the title before the campaign reached the halfway point. A freak
mechanical breakage in France delivered the second and last DNF whereas
Everts' only non-score (in three years) was 'Pichon-induced' in South Africa.
The twenty-eight-year-old never left the podium in the latter part of 2004 but
Everts was always by his side. A rider with incredible technical talent and a
whirlwind force over a single lap (fourteen pole positions) Pichon is always a
fascinating sight on the race track. Aggressive, fearless and demanding of his
team with regards to the set-up and feel of the bike, he is the fastest rider in the
world when the track suits him and self-imposed pressure to perform does not
disrupt his concentration.

3. Ben Townley (New Zealand)

Red Bull Champ KTM

GP wins: 9

Moto wins: 21

Podiums: 9

World Championship pos: 1st (MX2)

Titles: 1, MX2

Ben is one of the hardest-working riders in the paddock and his strength and
ability to get the best out of the KTM 250 prototype made him virtually unbeatable
in 2004. He was ruthless in the sand and equally quick on various other terrain.
When the GP circus arrived in town, the good money would always be on Townley
before a wheel had even turned.

BT missed the podium only seven times from sixteen races. When he had a
mechanical problem (only three from the six DNFs were his fault) he managed to
win the other moto on the same day. The Italian Grand Prix was the only round
where Townley did not manage a top-three result in either race. Friendly and
seemingly on good terms with ninety-nine per cent of the paddock and people
inside the sport, Townley is one of the more popular riders and always has

time for everyone. The nineteen-year-old was persuaded to stay in the World Championships for 2005. He will move up to the MX1 class where he will be able to take on Everts, whose style, many have commented, Townley replicates admirably.

4. Antonio Cairoli (Italy)
De Carli Yamaha
GP wins: 1
Moto wins: 1
Podiums: 5
World Championship pos: 3rd (MX2)
Titles: 0

The surprise element of the 2004 World Championships, rookie Antonio Cairoli deserves his lofty placing in this list by sheer talent and confidence alone. He beat fellow countrymen, with ten times more experience, like Chiodi, Bartolini, Federici and Stevanini. His persistent chase of Townley, Rattray and Sword throughout the season also shed light on a hungry will and determination that were just a couple of his positive attributes.

The eighteen-year-old may not be the most photogenic rider off the bike but he is definitely one of the more spectacular on the motorcycle. Cairoli often played with the Yamaha 4-stroke like it was a BMX and this flair singled him out for attention immediately. His slight frame assisted enormously with a propensity to gain holeshots and this advantage on sand, hard-pack or deep mud meant he was always looking for podiums. Naturally there were some rough edges and his season was by no means a breeze; the non-qualification in Great Britain (a track he should have relished) was a disappointment. However, a breakthrough like his does not come around every year and for 2005 he starts as one of the red-hot favourites for regular GP victories.

5. Kevin Strijbos (Belgium)
Team Suzuki
GP wins: 0
Moto wins: 2
Podiums: 2
World Championship pos: 5th (MX1)
Titles: 0

If Cairoli was the young star of MX2 then Strijbos was the shining light of MX1. Still a teenager, Strijbos completed only his third season of Grand Prix racing in 2004 and did so by defeating some of the sport's biggest names and developing the Suzuki RM-Z 450 at the same time. Strijbos was left to carry the factory team when Joel Smets stepped back at the halfway point. Kevin was never flustered by the responsibility and consistently placed the Suzuki inside the top five, taking two moto wins in dominant fashion and also his debut GP podium at Lichtenvoorde. Kevin's inexperience meant that he was still not ready for a Championship challenge (and technically neither was the Suzuki in '04) but his unrelenting pursuit of more established riders such as Everts, Pichon, Jorgensen, Melotte and Ramon was surprising. Kevin was not fast at every track and sometimes didn't have the stamina to push strong at the end of each moto but he finished the longest season of his career with a lot of praise, high opinion and of course a debut Motocross of Nations winners' medal. Seemingly always smiling, Strijbos has matured mentally and physically. The awkward and gangly teenager was effectively replaced by a confident young man who knew he was often in exalted company at the front of the field and had every right to be there.

6. Tyla Rattray (South Africa)

Red Bull Champ KTM
GP wins: 3
Moto wins: 1
Podiums: 8
World Championship pos: 2nd (MX2)
Titles: 0

Tyla's season was full of ups and downs. One week he would take his debut GP win and next be fighting for a top-ten position. In some ways he was at a disadvantage immediately, riding the 125cc 2-stroke, but then he was steering the machine that had taken three World Championships in the last four years and was one of the pure factory motorcycles on the line. Rattray made the most of his position, and his tenacity while often riding with injury problems was a redeeming feature. Sometimes qualification would be a fraught experience and he was no stranger to the Last Chance session but, having trained and spent a lot of time alongside Townley, he was one of the few that could challenge the World Champion on a semi-regular basis. The eighteen-year-old crashed a lot but then he was also fast enough to pick up the pieces when the direction of a race would suddenly change; hence his three GP wins but only one moto victory.

Rattray's on-track self-assurance was matched by a growing esteem in the paddock and towards the press. Always ready with a cheeky comment; his goading of Townley at the South African Saturday evening press conference was priceless.

7. Stephen Sword (Great Britain)

Kawasaki Racing Team
GP wins: 1
Moto wins: 2
Podiums: 5
World Championship pos: 4th (MX2)
Titles: 0

Stephen Sword would most probably like to slice the 2004 World Championship in half and remember the first part. The likeable Scot lifted himself to the status of Britain's top Grand Prix rider this year with two moto wins, a GP victory and five podiums in the opening seven rounds. Before 2004 he had struggled to post top-five results but then found himself championship leader after five races. The reasons for the transformation had been his first factory contract with Kawasaki and Jan de Groot's Eindhoven-based team, and a dedicated push on all aspects of his riding towards achieving his Grand Prix dreams after cleaning-up on the 125cc British national scene.

Sword's early success was a revelation to all, but after an excellent podium at the British Grand Prix his campaign began to fall apart. The new Kawasaki KX 250F proved to be a delicate creature and often refused to function, sometimes dramatically throwing the twenty-four-year-old to the ground. He was lucky to escape serious injury in Italy, Belgium and Germany. Contracting an energy-sapping virus around the time of Loket was like kicking the man while he was down. Sword would go on to finish fourth overall, missing his aim of a top-three slot, but the manner of his exciting challenge to Townley in South Africa served as a reminder of what he will be capable of in 2005.

8. Josh Coppins (New Zealand)

CAS Honda
GP wins: 1
Moto wins: 2
Podiums: 9
World Championship pos: 3rd (MX1)
Titles: 0

Josh Coppins has been through the sporting mill in the last three years.
After being World Championship challenger to Pichon (2002), enduring a doping saga, the Vismara team collapse and finally a broken ankle and back after a 2003 supercross crash (almost ending his career and still causing him to walk with a limp), his debut Grand Prix victory on the Isle of Wight became an even sweeter achievement after nearly ten seasons.

The twenty-seven-year-old started and finished 2004 very strongly but seemed to lose his way after the British Grand Prix, as if all that excruciating and pent-up desire to win had been sucked out of him, never to return. It took several GPs for the iron will to resurface and the bleak spell where he seemed to be saying every week that his riding was 'poor' or 'not good enough' distanced him to a third-placed outcast where he could not really breach the twosome of Everts and Pichon like he had on the Island. Coppins is a physical rider and also one of the authentic nice guys in the paddock. His long-overdue win was applauded by many, showing the high regard in which this constant servant to the sport is held.

9. Tanel Leok (Estonia)
Motovision Racing Suzuki
GP wins: 0
Moto wins: 0
Podiums: 0
World Championship pos: 6th (MX1)
Titles: 0

Tanel Leok only scored a single top-three moto result in 2004, but he started the season racing a stock Suzuki RM250cc 2-stroke for the small British Motovision team and finished as a Kawasaki works rider for 2005 with the label of the most-promising MX1 newcomer.

A nineteen-year-old of few words, the Estonian keeps himself to himself but is a powerhouse on the track and brings an all-guns-blazing style to the GP series. After a few rounds to get the hang of the Suzuki, Leok started increasing his pace and running with the group in contention for top-five positions despite the technical limitations. Leok was unstoppable and his efforts attracted the attention of Suzuki bosses who upgraded the 250 to a works 450. Mechanical trouble during the first moto robbed Leok of a sure-fire debut podium in Ireland.

Blissfully free of obligation while in the comfy confines of Motovision, how Leok will handle a factory team environment and the demands that will be made on his untested technical knowhow remains to be seen for 2005.

10. Steve Ramon (Belgium)
Red Bull KTM
GP wins: 0
Moto wins: 1
Podiums: 4
World Championship pos: 4th (MX1)
Titles: 1, 125 (2003)

Many people forgot that Steve was a defending World Champion in 2004. Quiet and hardly outgoing, Ramon is one of those riders who just blends into the background of the paddock. For large chunks of 2004 he was also fairly invisible on the track, often starting well but slipping back into mid-top-ten obscurity by the end of the motos. The twenty-four-year-old did make a bold statement with some of his results, even if his riding often came under criticism for being a little lightweight. He was 2003 125 World Champion and by the end of 2004 had taken a moto victory, several podiums and became a double Motocross of Nations winner. In his debut season he also had to bear the pressure of being the sole factory KTM rider in the premier class after Gunderson's knee injury.

Ramon is often very serious but there were signs that the frosty façade could easily melt. He smiled a lot more as the year went on and was jovial with the press. On the track he is a cool customer and rides conservatively; the fact that he is regarded as the future of Belgian motocross (together with Strijbos) shows that he is part of a very strong pedigree. His win in Zolder was the highlight and he achieved his goal of a top-five finish overall.

Tech Specs
Stars of the MX1 and MX2 World Championship

Although largely based on production models, the factory teams in MX1 used an array of special parts for the racing motorcycles. Titanium and carbon components down to the smallest nut and bolt all helped to reduce weight, while inside the engines some modifications were made to squeeze the best power and driveability for Grand Prix racing.

MX1

Yamaha YZ450FM (Stefan Everts, Yamaha L&M Motocross Team)

Engine type: 449cc single-cylinder liquid-cooled 4-stroke, DOHC 5-valve.

Carburetion: Single Keihin FCR 41mm carburettor.

Lubrication: Semi-pressurized wet sump.

Maximum power: 58hp.

Ignition: YRRD computer-adjustable CDI.

Transmission: 4-speed.

Clutch: Hydraulic, wet with 10 plates.

Frame: Steel semi-double cradle.

Front suspension: Factory fully adjustable 50mm upside-down Kayaba forks.

Rear suspension: Monocross with Factory Kayaba gas shock absorber.

Front brake: 270mm single disc, Brembo Radial calliper.

Rear brake: 245mm single disc. Weight: 102kg. Fuel capacity: 8 litres.

Honda CRF 450R (Josh Coppins, CAS Honda)

Engine type: 449cc liquid-cooled single-cylinder 4-stroke.

Carburetion: Keihin 40mm flat slide.

Ignition: Solid-state CD with electronic advance.

Transmission: Close-ratio 5-speed.

Front suspension: 47mm inverted Showa cartridge fork with 16-position rebound and 16-position compression-damping adjustability; 12.4 inch travel.

Rear suspension: Pro-Link Showa single-shock with spring preload, 17-position rebound-damping adjustability and compression-damping adjustment separated into two-speed (13 positions) and high-speed (3.5 turns); 12.6 inch travel.

Front brake: Single 240mm disc with twin-piston calliper.

Rear brake: Single 240mm disc. Wheelbase: 58.5 inches.

Seat height: 37.6 inches. Ground clearance: 13.4 inches.

Dry weight: 100kg. Fuel capacity: 7.5 litres.

KTM 450 SX 4-Stroke (Kenneth Gundersen, Red Bull KTM)

Engine: 449,39cc single-cylinder liquid-cooled 4-stroke.

Performance: approx. 56hp.

Transmission: 4 gears.

Carburettor: Keihin MX FCR 41.

Lubrication: Pressure lubrication with 2 Eaton pumps.

Clutch: Wet multi-disc clutch, operated hydraulically.

Ignition: Kokusan digital CDI.

Frame: Chromium molybdenum.

Subframe: Titanium. Front suspension: WP-USD 52 MA.

Rear suspension: WP-PDS shock absorber. Front brakes: Disc brake 260mm.

Rear brakes: Disc brake 220mm. Steering head angle: 63.5°.

Wheelbase: 1,481±10mm. Fuel capacity: approx. 7 litres.

Weight: approx. 100kg.

Suzuki RM-Z 450: (Joel Smets, Team Suzuki)

Engine: 450cc single-cylinder 4-stroke, water-cooled.

Power: 60+ @ 9,000+ rpm.

Valve: DOHC FOUR-VALVE. Carburetion: Keihin FCR.

Lubrication: Semi-dry sump. Clutch: Wet multi plates.

Transmission: 4-speed constant mesh.

Frame: Twin-spar aluminium alloy.

Front suspension: Inverted telescopic.

Rear suspension: New Link. Tyres: Pirelli.

Brakes: Single disc (steel). Length: 2,175mm.

Width: 815mm. Height: 1,270mm. Wheelbase: 1,490mm.

Weight: 98kg. Fuel: 7.5 litres.

Aprilia MXV 4.5 (Javier Garcia Vico, Aprilia Racing)

Engine: 449cc 77° V-twin liquid cooling with centrifugal pump.

Timing system: Single overhead shaft controlled by a silent chain; four titanium valves per cylinder.

Maximum revs: 14,000 rpm.

Frame type: Perimetrical, made of steel with alloy mounting.

Gearbox: Front clutch with 4 gears.

Clutch: Multiple-disc wet clutch with hydraulic control.

Ignition: Digital electronic.

Lubrication: Double separate lubrication with external tank.

Shock absorber: 'Sachs'.

Front brake: 2-pistons floating calliper, braking disc 270.

Rear brake: 1-piston floating calliper, braking disc 240.

Tyres: Pirelli.

Exhaust: Central 'Leo Vince X3'.

Fuel-tank capacity: 8.5 litres.

motocross
2004 Grand Prix Review

MX2

Yamaha YZ250FM (Andrew McFarlane, Bike...It Yamaha Dixon Racing)

Engine type: 249cc single-cylinder liquid-cooled 4-stroke, DOHC 5-valve.

Ignition: YRRD computer-adjustable CDI.

Carburetion: Keihin FCR 38/41mm.

Lubrication system: Semi-pressurised wet sump

Maximum power: 49ps+.

Transmission: 5-speed.

Primary drive: Gear.

Clutch: Wet multi-plate.

Final drive: Chain.

KTM 250 SX 4-stroke (Marc de Reuver, Red Bull Champ KTM)

Engine: 249,61cc single-cylinder liquid-cooled 4-stroke.

Performance: 42hp.

Transmission: 6 gears.

Carburettor: Keihin MX FCR 37.

Lubrication: Pressure lubrication with 2 Eaton pumps.

Clutch: Wet multi-disc clutch, operated hydraulically.

Ignition: Kokusan digital CDI.

Frame: Chromium molybdenum.

Subframe: Titanium.

Front suspension: WP-USD 52 MA.

Rear suspension: WP-PDS shock absorber.

Suspension travel front/rear: 300/335mm.

Front brakes: Disc brake 260mm.

Rear brakes: Disc brake 220mm.

Steering head angle: 63°.

Wheelbase: 1,461±10mm.

Fuel capacity: approx. 7 litres.

Weight: approx. 95kg.

Honda CRF 250R (Jamie Dobb, RWJ Honda)

Engine: 249cc liquid-cooled single-cylinder 4-stroke.

Carburation: Keihin 37mm flat slide with throttle-position sensor.

Ignition: Solid-state CD with electronic advance.

Transmission: Close-ratio 5-speed.

Front suspension: 47mm inverted Showa cartridge fork with 16-position rebound and 16-position compression-damping adjustability; 12.4 inch travel.

Rear suspension: Pro-Link Showa single-shock with spring-preload, 17-position rebound-damping adjustability, and compression-damping adjustment separated into two-speed (13 positions) and high-speed (3.5 turns); 12.6 inch travel.

Front brake: Single 240mm disc with twin-piston calliper.

Rear brake: Single 240mm disc.

Wheelbase: 1,478.2mm.

Dry weight: 93.6kg.

Fuel capacity: 7.5 litres.

Kawasaki KX250F (Mickael Maschio, Kawasaki Racing Team)

Engine: 249cc liquid-cooled, 4-stroke.

Valve/Induction system: DOHC, 4 valves.

Maximum power: 31.7 kW {43.1 PS}/ 11,000 rpm (production version).

Carburettor: Keihin FCR37.

Ignition: Digital AC-CDI.

Transmission: 5-speed, return.

Frame type: Perimeter, high-tensile steel with D-section tubes for upper frame rails.

Rake/Trail: 26.5°/110mm.

Front suspension: 48mm upside-down cartridge-type telescopic fork.

Rear suspension: New Uni-Trak with adjustable preload.

Front-wheel travel: 300mm.

Rear-wheel travel: 310mm.

Front brakes: Single semi-floating 250mm disc, dual-piston calliper.

Rear brakes: Single 240mm disc, single-piston calliper.

Dimensions (L x W x H): 2,170 x 840 x 1,270mm.

Wheelbase: 1,475mm.

Fuel capacity: 7.5 litres.

Dry weight: 92.5kg.

round one
Grand Prix of Flanders
Zolder, 20-21 March 2004

round one
Grand Prix of Flanders
Zolder, 20-21 March 2004

As a cold, hard wind battered the paddock in Belgium, where the teams and riders had gathered for the first of sixteen races in the 2004 World Championships, it was hard not to draw a parallel to the shifting times of motocross. A new force had swept into Grand Prix. While the swirling Belgian breeze wrecked PA equipment, the jet-wash bay and gave the team awnings a lively dance, it remained to be seen whether the reinstated 'powers-that-be' would have an equally uprooting affect with their new policies and ploys for the future.

The permanent motor sport facility of Zolder was again a significant venue for motocross. Just six months earlier Ricky Carmichael defeated Stefan Everts at the fifty-seventh MX of Nations, even if the Belgians did go on to record their thirteenth victory in the competition. Now Youthstream had selected the early staged Grand Prix of Flanders to open another era for the sport and were not shy to face the packed press room in a public declaration of their new term. Behind the professional presentation around Zolder and claims by Giuseppe Luongo that he wanted to make motocross 'great again' there hid a darker story. In reaction to the prize-money cuts that Youthstream had implemented, involving payment only to the top ten finishers and with a view towards the system being scrapped altogether in 2005, the riders had called an all-too-rare meeting on Saturday with new factory Suzuki rider and 2003 650 World Champion Joel Smets as the motivating force. It seemed that some sort of demonstration was likely; a signed petition at least would be presented in complaint. Background activities had obviously been whirring by the time Mr Luongo had taken the microphone for a

KTM Carnival? Ben Townley leads teammate Marc de Reuver during a chilly Zolder weekend.

lengthy speech in which he said one of his main focuses was to keep the young talent in GPs instead of the fashionable switch to the more lucrative US AMA series. His reference to the fact that 'We cannot have thirty-four-year-olds winning Grand Prix, I am not interested in this,' could be seen as a direct jibe at Smets; matching exactly the veteran's age as one of the more senior riders in the MX1 class. Sure enough later on, Smets confirmed his dissatisfaction with the regime on behalf of the riders when he slammed the notion that potential stars operating on a shoestring budget would not be able to exist in GPs if scoring two decent eleventh positions in a World Championship race on the other side of Europe would not result in a single Euro. The ever-talkative Belgian provided the highlight of the war-of-words, though, when he paused mid-question to answer his mobile, a call from his wife to find when he was coming back to the motor home for dinner. The ever-savvy Smets deliberately tacked on a 'love you too' to the end of the conversation, much to the amusement of his audience and to continue his long running charm-offensive with the press.

Both parties had their rationale and it was hard to find fault with the perspectives, even if perhaps it was Youthstream's duty and responsibility to unite the paddock and source the apparent funding problem by their own means. It was equally difficult to see where the power lay and who had the capabilities to obtain their goals without the whole thing 'kicking-off'. Youthstream and the FIM were the ringmasters but the riders were the stars of the show and what the punters were paying to see in the first place. Zolder not only represented the opening race of the new MX1 and MX2 World Championship but also the first round in a lengthy bout between the factions that would simmer under the surface for most of the season.

The motocross circuit at Zolder was sprawled over sections of the asphalt and adjacent to the pits, press centre and paddock. In terms of infrastructure Zolder

The MX1 World Championship is born but Zolder was not to be a fantastic meeting for either Mickael Pichon (2) or Stefan Everts (72). Steve Ramon (11) was a first moto winner.

Pichon was the victim of crashes in both motos and was playing catch-up to the leaders.

would not be bettered in the 2004 calendar. The GP track hadn't changed much in layout since the Nations. The entirely man-made, sandy and technical course became extremely rough as the cold and rainy weekend wore on and the World Championships could not have begun with a more gruelling and testing terrain. The sand was soft and the jumps started to erode; the slightest lack of concentration would spell disaster. The combination of nerves and the demands of the circuit often caught out the best riders, making the Grand Prix something of an open affair and certainly difficult to predict. The highlights were the immense finish-line jump and the swirling cambered 'S' section that led up to the whoops, akin to a giant sand-bunker.

Saturday

In the MX2 class, KTM had unveiled their potent lineup of stars on the Friday evening, and the assault consisting of Marc de Reuver, Ben Townley and Tyla Rattray (although without fourth member Erik Eggens who was going to miss another season through a serious back injury) set about making an instant impression during the qualifying heats. The MX2 contest normally supplies the main point of interest on a Saturday as the forty-minute pre-qualifying morning session determines the ranking for the two twenty-minute and two-lap races in the afternoon. The top twelve finishers from both heats, along with the fastest six riders from a 'Last Chance' chrono at the end of the day, complete the thirty entrants for the MX2 gate. The complicated procedure allows every opportunity possible for youthful, fast and unsigned talent to make an impression and become part of the select 'thirty'. With the winner of the first qualification race earning pole and the victor of the second heat taking to the line in second, the orders are spliced accordingly.

The mantra that would be echoed throughout the season by the riders was the need to obtain a decent start in the motos to prevent the factory boys winning the race before it was barely a lap old. Therefore Saturday's schedule was often a fiercely contested one, with each metre behind the start gate counting more favourably towards that crucial dive into the first corner. De Reuver satisfied most of the expectant pre-season punditry by winning the first heat by almost a minute and a half over Manuel Monni. Townley made it an orange double immediately afterwards but had to overtake early 'holeshotter', number '222', who, after a quick revision of the programme, revealed himself as Antonio Cairoli. He would go on to play an important and leading role in the MX2 2004 World Championship saga. Honda were making a refreshed bow in MX2 with the new CRF 250F, campaigned by ex-World Champion Jamie Dobb, Jeff Dement and Carl Nunn. Dement was the highest placed with fourth in the second heat. Special mention must also go to talented young Spaniard Jonathan Barragan, riding a stock 125cc KTM 2-stroke. Although the teenager finished some seventeen seconds behind Townley, his resourcefulness proved that the 125cc machines could still be a match for the 4-strokes. The Last Chance session (very much 'last chance saloon') was unusually populated with star names. Rattray, factory Kawasaki rider and Britain's top prospect Stephen Sword, new RTT Honda team representative Nunn, Tom Church, Kosak KTM teenage hopeful Aigar Leok, three-times former World Champion Alessio Chiodi and rising French star Sebastien Pourcel were just a few that were foiled by the heat events, whether due to mechanical reasons

Defending MX2 World Champion Ramon produced a hefty shock at his first race in the senior class.

or human error, causing the top-twelve cut-off bracket to be missed. Chiodi, one of those anticipated to challenge for the MX2 crown, was forced out of action because of a broken hand, apparently sustained after slipping getting out of the shower.

In MX1 Mickael Pichon took to the track in the unfamiliar red of Honda after winning comprehensively for the last three years in the yellow and blue of Suzuki. The most successful Frenchman in the history of motocross was also steering a 450cc 4-stroke for the first time after his untimely sacking from the Belgian-based Suzuki team towards the end of 2003, a mere fortnight after he had damaged knee ligaments and would be facing five months of rehabilitation. Many were curious to see the level of speed Pichon would be capable of at the opening GP as a consequence of a hefty period away from the bike, and were not

disappointed as the twenty-eight-year-old flicked the Tiscali Honda around the Belgian leaps during the thirty-minute qualifying session to seal what would be the first of many pole positions during the year.

The members of the victorious Belgian Motocross of Nations team were all facing their own personal dilemmas. Reigning Champion Stefan Everts had crashed while contesting the first round of the Belgian Championship in the week leading up to the Grand Prix and was nursing a damaged rib. Joel Smets was in a worse state, having broken the anterior cruciate ligament in his right knee at an international meeting in Mantova a month prior. The five times 'number one' had trained hard in order to make his Suzuki debut at Zolder, but a decent result wasn't realistically expected. Steve Ramon, the current 125cc World Champion, was making his first steps into the bigger class riding the factory KTM and was

Stefan Everts recorded his worst results since the start of the millennium but was hampered by a rib injury.

Sunday

The sense of 'lottery' that had surrounded the build-up and practice sessions permeated race day as the four motos of thirty-five minutes and two-lap duration provided some dramatic scenes. The first MX2 race kicked off the 2004 World Championship season. True to form, Marc de Reuver repeated his sensational speed from Saturday and lapped almost half the field, with Townley not able to close on his teammate. De Reuver's first haul of 25 points for his title purse was made even more impressive by the fact that he suffered rear brake trouble for the majority of the moto. Cairoli started well again (indeed, he would holeshot both times) but signs of inexperience crept in when he faded from a first-lap position of second to fifth, and then crashed midway through the race. Andrew McFarlane (Yamaha), Dobb and Sword rounded out a top five that contained four different manufacturers. The KTMs looked to have the upper edge, although there were whispers of reliability problems lurking in the background waiting to be proven accurate.

The first surprise of the day arrived in the next MX2 event just after lunch, as de Reuver hit a fallen Pascal Leuret on the first lap and received a face full of Belgian sand. The lanky Dutchman, who often makes no secret of his emotions on the bike, remounted and ripped through the field like a strong Flemish gust and amazingly climbed from twenty-fifth to third place just nine laps later, only to crash again and finally rescue fourth spot, finishing just behind Aigar Leok who was a dizzying third for the 2-stroke brigade. Townley happily led from the gate without distraction as Sword's highest ever GP moto result culminated in his debut podium and an excellent start to his career as a Kawasaki rider.

So far, so KTM, and a pleasing one-two for the Orange boys. 'I have learnt a lot over the three years and today I was patient after seeing Marc far ahead in the first moto,' said overall victor Townley. 'In the second race I got a good start and went for it. I enjoyed the two motos. It's been a brilliant GP.'

If the Austrians thought their results couldn't get any better then Ramon blasted from the line to shock the flocks of excited fans and the contents of the Zolder paddock in the first ever MX1 contest. The twenty-four-year-old took advantage of early leader Pichon's slow-speed tumble after losing the front end of the Honda through the 'S' section on lap two, and Suzuki's Kevin Strijbos also suffering a crash while leading going through the whoops only two circulations deeper into the race, to front the field and stretch away to his debut MX1 success. The normally staid Belgian was all smiles and the premature doubts that were pointed towards his fitness and capability of beating the world's best (luck-assisted or not) were instantly hushed. Strijbos would angrily dump the redundant prototype

naturally feeling the pressure, although there was a common understanding within the large Austrian team that 2004 would be a learning year.

Factory Honda rider Gordon Crockard, one of the very few to beat Pichon in the old 250cc class, was an early casualty. The luckless Irishman had snapped a knee ligament the week previously at the opening round of the British Championships and although able to walk, was not fit to race. He qualified twenty-fifth but then packed his bag on Saturday evening for an operation that would see him miss most of the season. The new Aprilias had not made their deadline and, with the members of the Corrado Maddi-led squad keeping tight-lipped about the project, it was left to rumour to suggest that the bike would not be GP-ready until round five in Germany. It was a small disappointment for Youthstream who had been trumpeting the inclusion of the Italian manufacturer and their controversial plans for a twin engine. The team elected to run Javier Garcia Vico and Thomas Traversini on blacked-out Hondas to at least maintain a presence and give their riders some track time.

450cc Suzuki a few laps later after his spill, while Pichon, clearly riding on the limit, jostled briefly with his teammate Brian Jorgensen for second place before being passed by Everts' factory Yamaha teammate Cedric Melotte, himself a 'crashee' within the first ten minutes of the race. Ramon produced a mature and error-free performance while it seemed those all around were negotiating some private turmoil. Stefan Everts fell in a moto for the first time in several seasons after colliding with James Noble in the whoops, but steadily made his way back to the top five. Smets went down in the first corner but ploughed away at the rear of the pack to secure thirteenth.

The carnage rolled on into the second moto. An opening-turn pile-up amazingly scooped Everts and Pichon amongst the melee. Pichon dramatically shielded himself on the ground, wary of his recent ill-luck with injury. Everts had now hit the deck more times in one meeting than since the start of the millennium. Both riders naturally embarked on a point-salvaging operation, with Everts saving fifth in spite of an injured thumb, and Pichon arriving in eleventh. Honda's Josh Coppins was an early leader just in front of a psyched Strijbos going for his first ever top-three finish, Garcia Vico was a surprising presence with the leaders as Ramon hovered in fourth. Cedric Melotte eventually seized a well-deserved overall win (only his second career victory) after passing Coppins on lap eight of nineteen. The podium was rounded out by Ramon and Coppins for an unlikely champagne-celebratory lineup at the first GP.

The on-track occurrences at Zolder led many to believe that a new dawn had blown in early with the wind. The latest MX1 generation, Strijbos, Ramon, Melotte and Kenneth Gundersen, had all played a significant role in the proceedings while the expected favourites of Everts, Pichon, Smets and Bervoets floundered at Flanders like their junior peers were 'supposed' to. 'The second race was just perfect. I thought I had moved into the lead too early when I passed Coppins but I resisted the pressure. Winning here was a big surprise for me,' confirmed Melotte. 'I had a little bit of luck on my side but this is the best motivation for the rest of the season. Of course I will not hesitate if I can produce some more surprises!'

MX2 witnessed the Grand Prix 'birth' of Cairoli, Leok and Sword while old-hands like Bartolini, Chiodi, Federici, Maschio and Dobb were nowhere to be seen near the top of the fresh championship points table. Despite the fact that Zolder was a unique track regarding the level of difficulty, and couldn't be considered too literally as an accurate forerunner for the rest of the campaign, several small trends for the championship term ahead were able to surface. The

The MX1 hordes hurry down to the first corner in Belgium where Pichon and Everts would quickly be caught in the mix.

considerably beefed-up Townley ignited a lengthy slow-burning fuse towards his title dream while Sword surprised his followers and would continue to do so in both good ways and bad. Cairoli and Strijbos were the new holeshot 'kings' and Coppins was, as ever, one of the few very consistent bets for the podium.

The first of five visits to the Benelux region passed efficiently and impressively. The promoter's decision to commence the World Championships at the best-equipped circuit launched the new-look Grand Prix series on the right foot. It was a shame the weather couldn't have been kinder but, then again, it was about to get much worse...

motocross
2004 Grand Prix Review

MX1

Overall Position	No.	Rider	Nat.	Bike	Race 1 Pos (Pts)	Race 2 Pos (Pts)	Total
1	7	Melotte, Cedric	BEL	Yamaha	2 (22)	1 (25)	47
2	11	Ramon, Steve	BEL	KTM	1 (25)	4 (18)	43
3	31	Coppins, Joshua	NZL	Honda	7 (14)	2 (22)	36
4	72	Everts, Stefan	BEL	Yamaha	5 (16)	5 (16)	32
5	2	Pichon, Mickael	FRA	Honda	3 (20)	11 (10)	30
6	10	Gundersen, Kenneth	NOR	KTM	8 (13)	6 (15)	28
7	8	Jorgensen, Brian	DEN	Honda	4 (18)	14 (7)	25
8	40	Leok, Tanel	EST	Suzuki	9 (12)	10 (11)	23
9	3	Smets, Joel	BEL	Suzuki	13 (8)	7 (14)	22
10	34	Noble, James	GBR	Honda	12 (9)	9 (12)	21
11	24	Strijbos, Kevin	BEL	Suzuki	0	3 (20)	20
12	53	Cooper, Paul	GBR	Honda	6 (15)	0	15
13	18	Bervoets, Marnicq	BEL	Yamaha	0	8 (13)	13
14	12	Theybers, Danny	BEL	Yamaha	17 (4)	12 (9)	13
15	77	Kovalainen, Marko	FIN	Honda	10 (11)	0	11
16	6	Garcia Vico, Francisco	SPA	Honda	11 (10)	0	10
17	48	Burnham, Christian	GBR	KTM	0	13 (8)	8
18	26	Pyrhonen, Antti	FIN	Suzuki	16 (5)	18 (3)	8
19	27	Atsuta, Yoshitaka	JPN	Honda	15 (6)	19 (2)	8
20	97	Breugelmans, Sven	BEL	KTM	18 (3)	17 (4)	7
21	80	de Dijcker, Ken	BEL	Honda	14 (7)	0	7
22	45	Martin, Christophe	FRA	Yamaha	0	15 (6)	6
23	50	Hucklebridge, Mark	GBR	KTM	20 (1)	16 (5)	6
24	75	Dobes, Josef	CZE	Suzuki	19 (2)	0	2
25	21	Dini, Fabrizio	ITA	KTM	0	20 (1)	1
26	73	Traversini, Thomas	ITA	Honda	0	0	0
27	61	Kragelj, Saso	SLO	Yamaha	0	0	0
28	123	Oddenino, Enrico	ITA	TM	0	0	0
29	43	Meo, Antoine	FRA	Kawasaki	0	0	0
30	47	Ristori, Marc	SUI	Honda	0	0	0

MX2

Overall Position	No.	Rider	Nat.	Bike	Race 1 Pos (Pts)	Race 2 Pos (Pts)	Total
1	30	Townley, Ben	NZL	KTM	2 (22)	1 (25)	47
2	17	de Reuver, Marc	NED	KTM	1 (25)	4 (18)	43
3	19	Sword, Stephen	GBR	Kawasaki	5 (16)	2 (22)	38
4	15	McFarlane, Andrew	AUS	Yamaha	3 (20)	5 (16)	36
5	76	Leok, Aigar	EST	KTM	10 (11)	3 (20)	31
6	64	Dobb, James	GBR	Honda	4 (18)	12 (9)	27
7	71	Maschio, Mickael	FRA	Kawasaki	9 (12)	7 (14)	26
8	56	Priem, Manuel	BEL	Suzuki	11 (10)	10 (11)	21
9	118	Boissiere, Anthony	FRA	Yamaha	17 (4)	9 (12)	16
10	49	Goncalves, Rui	POR	Yamaha	8 (13)	18 (3)	16
11	16	Rattray, Tyla	RSA	KTM	0	6 (15)	15
12	55	Nunn, Carl	GBR	Honda	16 (5)	11 (10)	15
13	83	Barragan, Jonathan	SPA	KTM	6 (15)	0	15
14	68	Philippaerts, David	ITA	KTM	7 (14)	0	14
15	22	Federici, Claudio	ITA	Yamaha	0	8 (13)	13
16	52	Leuret, Pascal	FRA	KTM	15 (6)	14 (7)	13
17	65	Monni, Manuel	ITA	Yamaha	13 (8)	17 (4)	12
18	70	Church, Tom	GBR	Kawasaki	12 (9)	0	9
19	211	Mackenzie, Billy	GBR	Yamaha	0	13 (8)	8
20	87	Dement, Jeff	USA	Honda	14 (7)	0	7
21	222	Cairoli, Antonio	ITA	Yamaha	0	15 (6)	6
22	90	Pourcel, Sebastien	FRA	Kawasaki	0	16 (5)	5
23	60	Barreda, Joan	SPA	KTM	18 (3)	0	3
24	96	Bernardez, Aaron	SPA	Honda	0	19 (2)	2
25	92	Cherubini, Luca	ITA	Suzuki	19 (2)	0	2
26	38	van Daele, Marvin	BEL	Suzuki	0	20 (1)	1
27	202	Smith, Wayne	GBR	KTM	20 (1)	0	1
28	95	Nagl, Maximilian	GER	KTM	0	0	0
29	711	Allier, Tomas	FRA	Kawasaki	0	0	0
30	121	Salaets, Kristof	BEL	Honda	0	0	0

Grand Prix of Spain
Bellpuig, 27-28 March 2004

round two
Grand Prix of Spain
Bellpuig, 27-28 March 2004

The opening Grand Prix of the season started a rapid-fire three-consecutive-weekend streak of World Championship events. With haste the teams packed up in Zolder on Sunday evening to begin the sprint south to Catalunya, northern Spain, about an hour outside the picturesque city of Barcelona, to the popular Bellpuig circuit. Bellpuig is a fast, technical course, sloped on a hillside with large jumps. The step-ups and quick downhill bomb-hole provide some of the most scenic and spectacular sights in Grand Prix racing. For the fans, just as much as the riders, Bellpuig supplies a little of everything; high-speed turns with varying gradients, a mean set of whoops and grippy dirt that cuts up nicely thanks to the computer-controlled watering system that keeps the mud damp and 'churnable'. Simple really; the softer and deeper the dirt, the rougher it gets, offering more lines and better racing and more of a test for the GP stars. There had been a few revisions to the layout this year, the installation of some mini-speed jumps across sections of the track looked to add some variety to the lines. The best intentions of the club, however, were completely washed out by a late Spanish winter.

Torrential rain arrived midway through Saturday morning and did not stop for the next twenty-four hours. There were rumours that the race programme could be cut to one moto per class or the slim possibility that the event could be cancelled altogether, such was the debilitating effect of the excessive downpour on the track. The start straight was effectively underwater and to make matters worse the temperatures dropped to lower than five or six degrees and did not budge. The irony of the conditions at the Spanish Grand Prix was not lost on a lot of people and the riders were surprisingly perky; a job still had to be done.

The deluge of Bellpuig. Sebastien Pourcel struggles to retrieve his Kawasaki in the same mire that would claim Pichon on Sunday.

Despite all the added practical grief that swampish mud entails, it also means any chance of decent racing slithers down the drain. Just surviving the motos without crashing and having a bath in the ooze would be an achievement. The deep ruts and sticky mud, combined with the cold, was also a test for the machines and many 4-strokes were found wanting by the end of play on Sunday.

There were some interesting new kit designs making an appearance in the waiting zone before the riders went out to try and part the Bellpuig Sea. Stiff foam in all shapes and sizes transformed the majority of helmets into bizarre oddities. The added sculptures were applied in a vain effort to try and deflect the wide roosts of mud from sticking to the headwear and doubling the weight. Andrew McFarlane adopted a surreal guise, with black sponge blobs almost doubling the size of his lid and creating a 1970s look with big 'beard-like' additions. The Australian even went so far as to hang a tear-off piece of plastic at the edge of his peak. On race day an assortment of glove-wiping fashion emerged. Stefan Everts sported a deft set of little white towels (an appropriate colour) that looked as though he was circulating with his pockets inside-out, while Mickael Pichon plumped for a butcher's-style apron tucked into the front of his riding pants. The extra measures adopted for the track to cope with the 'barro' were a small theme of minor curiosity and amusement for all, although it is debateable if any were indeed effective.

There was little cause for humour on Friday evening as the riders met secretly in a freezing paddock to listen to Joel Smets' plans to gain dialogue with Youthstream bosses. With a single bright sodium lamp bathing the living area, one by one the shadows gathered from their motor homes. The majority were the under-represented young element but riders such as Kevin Strijbos, Brian Jorgensen, Mickael Pichon, Stefan Everts (who approached James Noble and asked him about the collision at Zolder causing the former to crash. Noble bluntly denied culpability) Jamie Dobb and a few other notable Grand Prix winners were present. As a friend of Everts and Smets, Ben Townley, arguably the brightest talent in the MX2 class, was lurking discretely near the back. Under instructions from KTM not to get involved in any political action, such as a potential strike, Townley at least showed solidarity to the cause. Some paperwork was passed around and a line formed to sign a petition objecting to the payment cuts. Smets was full of figures and research and announced that the prize fund had been sliced by more than half this season. Stefan Everts was allegedly given an audience by Giuseppe Luongo over the weekend but no action was taken by either side to resolve the differences. The factory stars do not depend on the race

The first-corner crash of the opening MX2 moto was particularly messy.

prizes as a wage but at least fifty per cent of the field, especially in MX2, need the potential income.

The meteorological dark clouds would clear for Sunday and even some belated sunshine would make an appearance. The first two motos of the day would still take place on heavily soggy mud, the likes of which hadn't been seen in the World Championships since perhaps the gunk of Genk in Belgium 2001. As ever the loyal and appreciative Spanish fans turned out in their thousands and although Bellpuig has seen better days, the Grand Prix still produced some memorable sights and upsets to push the 'Tombola' of the World Championships enthusiastically onwards.

Saturday

Of all the people walking around the paddock with three extra layers, virgin World Championship leader Cedric Melotte had an extra spring in his step. The Belgian, who speaks five languages, was also an expectant father and life was currently very rosy. His tune would change, however, by the time the chequered flag dropped on Sunday. Mickael Pichon had cause enough for optimism, considering he had won the premier class GP at Bellpuig for the last three consecutive

Top: Mickael Maschio drives the 250 up one of the step inclines that would later witness his undoing.
Bottom: Andrew McFarlane's foam attire was one of the more inventive additions.

seasons and had implemented something of a monopoly at the Catalan track. Stefan Everts also had fond memories. The thirty-one-year-old was chasing a seventy-third success and his latter career period of domination had begun in Spain with 500cc victory in 2001. Three World Championships and twenty-eight victories later, Everts, also an expectant father (they must have been bored in the L&M Yamaha squad over the winter), was looking to restart his 2004 plight for title number eight.

The whoops section is one of the most popular viewing spots at Bellpuig and it is also a fairly good location to judge technique. MX2 Kawasaki rider Sebastien Pourcel was an eye-catching performer through the difficult section during wet practice, keeping his 4-stroke throttle pinned and skimming over the small but daunting humps with an impressive speed. Pourcel would use this GP to enforce his Grand Prix potential, as would fellow rookie and Yamaha rider Cairoli. The teenage Italian's riding style was certainly flamboyant. Cairoli led the opening lap of the second heat and forged his way to the chequered flag with the bulbous-headed McFarlane in second and Pourcel third.

Marc de Reuver was again setting the pace, recording the fastest lap in pre-qualifying practice and then taking part in an entertaining battle with Townley in the first heat. Only a mistake from the twenty-one-year-old allowed Townley to take the win and his first pole of the season. KTM, of course, were returning to the circuit where the 250 4-stroke made a troubled debut twelve months earlier and clearly had not been up to the task in terms of reliability. After such a successful weekend at Zolder, KTM would be celebrating a different kind of victory on Sunday and it wouldn't involve either of their 250cc riders, as the 4-stroke developed stomach problems, probably remembering what an unpleasant experience the 2003 Spanish Grand Prix had been. Factory Kawasaki duo Sword and 2002 125cc World Champion Mickael Maschio completed an effective warm-up for what would be one of the best meetings of the year for the Dutch-based 'Green' team by finishing fourth and third respectively behind Townley and de Reuver.

Body warmers and jackets were not a rare sight on the track for the MX1 thirty-minute afternoon chrono. The times had slowed by some fourteen seconds after the initial morning outings as the course carved up into half-metre-sized ruts and berms. Kenneth Gundersen was quickest in both free practice sessions and looked oddly at home in the marsh; at last showing some threatening speed on the works KTM. The Norwegian was only three-tenths of a second behind Pichon, which was quite an accomplishment considering the Frenchman's almost unmatchable ability to clock a phenomenally fast single-lap time. Joel Smets

Stephen Sword headed for a second consecutive podium finish but admitted that survival was his only thought on Sunday.

was reasonably well placed in fifth, ahead of Coppins and behind Everts and Jorgensen, and feeling more confident despite the limited use of his knee. Zolder victor Melotte was more cautious and rested in ninth. The majority of the paddock and the few sodden spectators were glad to see the end of Saturday afternoon as the rain continued to soak the landscape.

Sunday

The mud wave took on tidal proportions as the MX2 riders rushed towards the first corner on Sunday morning. Inevitably there was a tangle and a splash but most of the protagonists came through unscathed if not cleanly. The rain had eased off halfway through the moto and not a moment too soon. The MX2 Grand Prix of Spain was a KTM topsy-turvy rollercoaster of luck with a handful of crashes thrown in and the Kawasaki boys playing an apt supporting role. Marc de Reuver was at the sharp end of the fortune scale. The KTM rider crashed in the whoops while second and closing in on the leader, before then embarrassingly toppling over while trying to retrieve his machine. Although he was able to come back to fourth place his teammate Townley had overtaken holeshotter Stephen Sword and escaped to win his second moto in succession extremely comfortably. Sword, Maschio and Rattray fought for second spot and the close encounter led to an incredible collision. Maschio held the advantage but lost control on lap fourteen of eighteen after cross-rutting the steep step-up. He veered across the track from his line on the far left, falling in the middle of the circuit. The hotly pursuing Sword was able to weave around his teammate but Rattray had no choice but to land directly on top of the Kawasaki, almost smacking Maschio in the process, and managing to bounce clear. The Frenchman's bike was too damaged to continue as Rattray regained his composure to beat Sword to the runner-up position. Aigar Leok created further positive impressions in his debut season, while local rider Barragan finished seventh and was amazingly the last rider not to be lapped.

With the dull sun and breeze helping to dry and stiffen the track there was less call for extreme anti-mud kit measures for the second moto. Maschio was out for vengeance after his poor luck in the first outing and never dropped out of the top two. The Kawasaki stalwart took his third consecutive chequered flag at the Spanish circuit but not before finally getting his slice of good fortune as de Reuver broke down in the whoops – hardly his favourite place on the track over the weekend – and Townley also suffered some mechanical trouble as well as a fall to retire from the race. Antonio Cairoli led a Grand Prix for the first time in his career but was also caught out by the slippery surface on lap four. Rattray crashed on the step-up in less dramatic fashion than the race-winner in the previous moto but was still able to take third position once de Reuver had confirmed his DNF with a flurry of fist-shaking at his lame machine. The second moto classification was like a reversal of roles; it seemed like everyone was destined for some good and bad results. Andrew McFarlane finished second behind Maschio which, combined with his initial sixth place, was good enough to mount the second step of the podium and confirm his first MX2 trophy. Sebastien Pourcel had a first moto to forget but was more proactive in the second and happily celebrated his best ever GP moto result so far with fourth. Only Sword and Rattray showed anything like Grand Prix-winning consistency and the eighteen-year-old South African gratefully, although somewhat bashfully, accepted his spoils. The

After a lacklustre weekend at Zolder, Everts uses his experience to beat Strijbos and take his first win of the year.

overall victory represented the first triumph for a 125cc 2-stroke in the class for almost a year but the handing of the 'red number plate' to the new World Championship leader in Stephen Sword saw a British rider head a title chase for the first time since 2001. If Rattray was inwardly over the moon then Sword must have been hovering on cloud nine, but seemingly took it all in his stride. When he acknowledged that there was still a long way to go it was very hard not to disagree, however euphoric the realisation of his double podium appearances must have felt.

The first zero on the score sheet for Townley came after a creditable opening moto win in Spain. Here he holds off Rattray.

The Stefan Everts of old was in residence for race day at Bellpuig. The MX1 class faced similar conditions to the MX2 riders for their first moto and the deep mud was especially harsh on Mickael Pichon as it sucked him into its grasp; literally. The Honda rider took a wide rut on the left-hander near the pits at the bottom of the watery hill and his 450 sank as he hit the slime, becoming lodged solid against two walls of mud. Dismounting, Pichon pushed and tugged at the bike like some Enduro rider caught in a bog but the wheel-less Honda wasn't to be freed. By now his Shark helmet was the size of a beach ball thanks to the thick roost of passing

riders. Disconsolately he had to admit defeat and climbed the pit barrier, walking back to the paddock in disbelief. At the front Kevin Strijbos again was quick off the mark. The Belgian inherited the lead after Jorgensen's Honda expired and started to construct a sizeable margin over his rivals. When victory looked assured halfway through the moto the eighteen-year-old was baulked and slowed by backmarkers, allowing the increasingly faster Everts to close. Once the pass was made on lap eleven of eighteen the mental damage was done and Strijbos could offer no resistance. Coppins also took advantage and was more decisive cutting his way through the lapped riders. Gundersen set himself up for a debut MX1 podium in fourth, while Vico gave cheer to the locals with a decent sixth in front of the improving Ken de Dijcker. Sixteen riders were lapped in total.

Strijbos was denied an overall top-three result in the second moto as his Suzuki locked-up exiting the whoops. The new machine was still producing some development gremlins and these hiccups cost Smets a lot of time and positions in the first race. This time the more senior of the teammates was able to enjoy a clear run. An excellent battle for fourth with former 500cc KTM sparring partner Vico took place, with Smets producing the overtaking move of the meeting by sliding up the inside of the Spaniard at the forty-five-degree right-hand first turn, full gas, bars on full lock. A risky pass but measured to perfection. Jorgensen had started well again and this time managed to keep upright on the driest mud the riders had experienced all weekend. Everts took the lead at more or less at the same point when he had passed Strijbos earlier in the day and maintained a cushion of several seconds over the Dane.

'I didn't expect to win this GP at all,' the Champion and new standings leader remarked. 'My rib injury is getting better but I tore some ligaments around my thumb and that made it difficult for me. In both races I was quite tense but managed to relax after about twenty minutes and win both heats, so that's a good step forward for the championship. It is good to see some new faces pushing for the lead and of course more interesting to have some new guys for me to race.' Again quiet consistency from Coppins, in a lonely third, meant another overall podium result and his most successful start to a World Championship in ten years. Melotte, meanwhile, was not able to adjust to the mud and a crash in both motos led to two disappointing top-ten finishes. Pichon completed what would be his worst weekend of the season after getting caught in the gate for the second moto. A furious thrash through nineteen positions in only three laps was an awesome sight and he finally claimed seventh in a state of rage. He did not know it at the time, but things were about to get much better for the Frenchman.

motocross
2004 Grand Prix Review

MX1

Overall Position	No.	Rider	Nat.	Bike	Race 1 Pos (Pts)	Race 2 Pos (Pts)	Total
1	72	**Everts, Stefan**	BEL	Yamaha	1 (25)	1 (25)	50
2	31	**Coppins, Joshua**	NZL	Honda	2 (22)	3 (20)	42
3	10	**Gundersen, Kenneth**	NOR	KTM	4 (18)	6 (15)	33
4	6	**Garcia Vico, Francisco**	SPA	Aprilia	5 (16)	5 (16)	32
5	3	**Smets, Joel**	BEL	Suzuki	9 (12)	4 (18)	30
6	11	**Ramon, Steve**	BEL	KTM	7 (14)	9 (12)	26
7	8	**Jorgensen, Brian**	DEN	Honda	0	2 (22)	22
8	7	**Melotte, Cedric**	BEL	Yamaha	10 (11)	10 (11)	22
9	40	**Leok, Tanel**	EST	Suzuki	8 (13)	12 (9)	22
10	80	**de Dijcker, Ken**	BEL	Honda	6 (15)	14 (7)	22
11	24	Strijbos, Kevin	BEL	Suzuki	3 (20)	0	20
12	74	Freibergs, Lauris	LAT	Honda	11 (10)	13 (8)	18
13	2	Pichon, Mickael	FRA	Honda	0	7 (14)	14
14	34	Noble, James	GBR	Honda	12 (9)	16 (5)	14
15	18	Bervoets, Marnicq	BEL	Yamaha	0	8 (13)	13
16	53	Cooper, Paul	GBR	Honda	18 (3)	11 (10)	13
17	26	Pyrhonen, Antti	FIN	Suzuki	16 (5)	18 (3)	8
18	45	Martin, Christophe	FRA	Yamaha	14 (7)	20 (1)	8
19	50	Hucklebridge, Mark	GBR	KTM	13 (8)	0	8
20	48	Burnham, Christian	GBR	KTM	0	15 (6)	6
21	27	Atsuta, Yoshitaka	JPN	Honda	15 (6)	0	6
22	85	Turpin, Vincent	FRA	Honda	20 (1)	17 (4)	5
23	43	Meo, Antoine	FRA	Kawasaki	17 (4)	0	4
24	21	Dini, Fabrizio	ITA	KTM	0	19 (2)	2
25	12	Theybers, Danny	BEL	Yamaha	19 (2)	0	2
26	77	Kovalainen, Marko	FIN	Honda	0	0	0
27	73	Traversini, Thomas	ITA	Honda	0	0	0
28	61	Kragelj, Saso	SLO	Yamaha	0	0	0
29	75	Dobes, Josef	CZE	Suzuki	0	0	0
30	123	Oddenino, Enrico	ITA	TM	0	0	0

MX1 World Championship standings:

Everts 82, Coppins 78, Melotte 69, Ramon 69, Gundersen 61, Smets 52, Jorgensen 47, Leok 45, Pichon 44, Garcia Vico 42, Strijbos 40, Noble 35, de Dijcker 29, Cooper 28, Bervoets 26, Freibergs 18, Pyrhonen 16, Theybers 15, Atsuta 14, Burnham 14, Hucklebridge 14, Martin 14, Kovalainen 11, Breugelmans 7, Turpin 5, Meo 4, Dini 3, Dobes 2.

MX2

Overall Position	No.	Rider	Nat.	Bike	Race 1 Pos (Pts)	Race 2 Pos (Pts)	Total
1	16	**Rattray, Tyla**	RSA	KTM	2 (22)	3 (20)	42
2	15	**McFarlane, Andrew**	AUS	Yamaha	6 (15)	2 (22)	37
3	19	**Sword, Stephen**	GBR	Kawasaki	3 (20)	5 (16)	36
4	71	**Maschio, Mickael**	FRA	Kawasaki	15 (6)	1 (25)	31
5	76	**Leok, Aigar**	EST	KTM	5 (16)	7 (14)	30
6	30	**Townley, Ben**	NZL	KTM	1 (25)	0	25
7	38	**van Daele, Marvin**	BEL	Suzuki	9 (12)	10 (11)	23
8	222	**Cairoli, Antonio**	ITA	Yamaha	14 (7)	6 (15)	22
9	112	**Cepelak, Jiri**	CZE	KTM	11 (10)	9 (12)	22
10	64	**Dobb, James**	GBR	Honda	8 (13)	12 (9)	22
11	83	Barragan, Jonathan	SPA	KTM	7 (14)	16 (5)	19
12	90	Pourcel, Sebastien	FRA	Kawasaki	0	4 (18)	18
13	17	de Reuver, Marc	NED	KTM	4 (18)	0	18
14	70	Church, Tom	GBR	Kawasaki	17 (4)	11 (10)	14
15	55	Nunn, Carl	GBR	Honda	0	8 (13)	13
16	68	Philippaerts, David	ITA	KTM	10 (11)	19 (2)	13
17	118	Boissiere, Anthony	FRA	Yamaha	13 (8)	17 (4)	12
18	114	Swanepoel, Garreth	RSA	KTM	20 (1)	13 (8)	9
19	5	Bartolini, Andrea	ITA	Yamaha	12 (9)	0	9
20	56	Priem, Manuel	BEL	Suzuki	0	14 (7)	7
21	41	Letellier, Antoine	FRA	Suzuki	0	15 (6)	6
22	69	Avis, Wyatt	RSA	Suzuki	16 (5)	0	5
23	92	Cherubini, Luca	ITA	Suzuki	0	18 (3)	3
24	87	Dement, Jeff	USA	Honda	18 (3)	0	3
25	37	Caps, Patrick	BEL	Yamaha	19 (2)	0	2
26	65	Monni, Manuel	ITA	Yamaha	0	20 (1)	1
27	49	Goncalves, Rui	POR	Yamaha	0	0	0
28	96	Bernardez, Aaron	SPA	Honda	0	0	0
29	52	Leuret, Pascal	FRA	KTM	0	0	0
30	202	Smith, Wayne	GBR	KTM	0	0	0
31	60	Barreda, Joan	SPA	KTM	0	0	0

MX2 World Championship standings:

Sword 74, McFarlane 73, Townley 72, de Reuver 61, Leok 61, Maschio 57, Rattray 57, Dobb 49, Barragan 34, Cairoli 28, Nunn 28, Boissiere 28, Priem 28, Philippaerts 27, van Daele 24, Pourcel 23, Church 23, Cepelak 22, Goncalves 16, Federici 13, Leuret 13, Monni 13, Dement 10, Bartolini 9, Swanepoel 9, Mackenzie 8, Letellier 6, Avis 5, Cherubini 5, Barreda 3, Caps 2, Bernardez 2, Smith 1.

round three
Grand Prix of Portugal
Agueda, 3-4 April 2004

round three
Grand Prix of Portugal
Agueda, 3-4 April 2004

Moving west to Portugal there was hope that the World Championships would find some better weather. The calendar also nudged into the first week of April as the series continued its onslaught. Agueda last entertained a Grand Prix back in 2000 and Mickael Pichon was the 250cc winner on that occasion. This would prove to be a telling omen and indeed end his eleven month absence from the top step.

The circuit was struggling to be ready for the third round of the season. Preparations had been ongoing since the start of the year but as the teams rolled through the downtrodden suburbs of Agueda, some eighty kilometres outside of Porto, they entered a facility that was still in the midst of transformation. The main problem, to everyone's dismay, was the venue's plight in coping with the deluge of rainfall. The voluminous Bellpuig clouds had followed the trucks across the Iberian Peninsula and were not about to let their 'prey' escape, even chucking in some hailstorms for good measure. The vastly separated and two-tiered paddock was in danger of flooding. The top section that housed the majority of the MX1 crews was mainly grass and saw a high compliment of standing water build up. The mechanics had to carve elaborate mini-channels and tunnelling systems in the turf to prevent the puddles seeping into the awning work areas. Circuit staff were working full-time, importing diggers of gravel and wood chippings to try and solidify the ground. The infrastructure, fitting in with the surroundings, was basic at best and the overall impression of the circuit was not one of high quality, which was a shame because the track itself was reasonably good.

Rookie Antonio Cairoli was quickly gaining attention for his exciting riding as much as the unforeseen results.

On Saturday morning, thankfully, the sunshine arrived and the rain stopped. The course, a reddish mix between sand and clay, began to dry immediately but was still very wet and became rougher with the wear of Saturday's action. The undulating layout was considerably different in comparison to recent years and a real effort had gone into converting the quarry setting into a fluid and technical prospect, even if it was still quite fast. Throughout practice and qualifying one solid line was predominant in certain sections but the water seemed to be evaporating quite well considering the recent quota and was a definite improvement over Bellpuig.

Three consecutive weeks of Grand Prix racing meant precious little time for riders to squeeze in testing time or recover from any injuries. The fortnight break after Agueda was eagerly anticipated by all. MX2 Championship leader Stephen Sword was one of those carrying a niggle after enduring the first two weeks with an ankle ailment. It was testimony to the hard work, extra strength and new confidence that Sword had brought to his riding that he was still able to post positive results. The twenty-four-year-old British Champion was clearly enjoying his status as a factory team member and the Kawasaki was proving to be up to the task of Grand Prix victories in its first season. The Scot was excellent in Sunday's second moto and although Ben Townley successfully erased the pain of Spain, Sword was the deserved headline-grabber as the first Brit to claim a chequered flag since Jamie Dobb conquered the 2002 125cc GP of Austria at the Karntenring. The Portuguese round was to be the last of the season for Paul Cooper. The injury-prone MX1 Honda rider would crash after running into the fallen Kenneth Gundersen's KTM on Sunday and break his collarbone in six places. In contrast the race saw Alessio Chiodi's return after missing out in Bellpuig and undergoing surgery in England to his fractured hand. Although the exciting potential of Cairoli and also McFarlane gave Yamaha cause for MX2 optimism they still depended on the resolute and proven form of riders like 'Chicco' and his countrymen Bartolini and Claudio Federici. The Japanese firm had won every single 125cc GP in the second half of 2003 thanks to Stefan Everts' efforts on the 250 and the bike was clearly vying with Honda for the most reliable machine in the category, but Kawasaki and KTM had done their homework. The class was a deliciously open affair and with two riders tied for the Championship lead after the proceedings in Portugal, appetites for further action were as wet as the Agueda paddock.

Top: Everts held off Pichon in the first moto but the Frenchman was irrepressible in the second race.
Bottom: Testing times for Suzuki… or rather a lack of them. Both Smets and Strijbos had difficulties in Agueda.

Saturday

Carl Nunn won the first qualification heat and Mickael Pichon did not take pole position; it was to be one of the more eyebrow-raising Saturdays of the season. Nunn gave the Honda its first taste of racetrack success by holeshotting the opening heat and maintaining a decent pace until the chequered flag. It was a surprising outcome and not one that many would have forecast, further adding to the pleasant jumble of the unexpected that the MX2 Championship was

divulging in its infancy. Nunn was naturally excited after his first pole for a number of years and in the wake of only setting the seventeenth-quickest time in pre-qualifying practice. A precarious talent that hadn't delivered the goods after his breakthrough 2000 season in the 125cc class, Nunn was showing long-overdue signs of a renaissance. The moto result hid the fact that de Reuver was charging and was clearly the fastest man on the track. The KTM rider had snapped his kick-start pedal in the formative stages and, not wishing to risk a stall, had taken his time to pass Sword, Chiodi and Bartolini. Once again it seemed as though de Reuver would be the main threat on Sunday even if behind closed doors his patience was wearing very thin with the temperamental 4-stroke machine.

Ben Townley's style on the 250 was visually and noticeably different. Softer and less aggressive, the New Zealander seemed to take more time and effort nursing the KTM and this factor may have accounted for the reduction of race-time mechanical glitches that were serially affecting the rev-happy de Reuver. Townley's riding bore marks of ritual practice in sand. His synergy with the KTM was a formidable package; a 'couple on honeymoon' compared to the 'divorcing mess' that de Reuver was inclined to experience. Townley had been suffering from sickness during the week but had little trouble disposing of the now-customary first-lap threat of Cairoli in the second heat and cleared off to win by some eighteen seconds. Unproven Frenchman Pascal Leuret, riding a 125cc KTM, took inspiration from Nunn's example and was placed third. Spanish GP winner Tyla Rattray was not enjoying his weekend so far and crashed behind the 'Nunn-show' to tip-toe unceremoniously into the Last Chance session for the second time in three weeks. Needless-to-say Rattray was still riding with the fresh buzz of his first GP victory and eased through the qualification back door with the quickest lap-time.

It was interesting to chart the progress of the German KTM Kosak team at this stage. Aigar Leok was already proving himself and looked more than capable of top-ten, touching top-five, race finishes. The other two youngsters, South African Gareth Swanepoel and Max Nagl, who's junior shoulders bore the brunt of Germany's motocross hopes, were on the borderline of qualification. Nagl did not make the grade in Portugal while 'Swanie' was last into the gate. With all three learning their trade on 125cc machinery the Grand Prix year was to be far from easy. By the end of the season, however, stretching into the Motocross of Nations, all three teenagers would have made vast improvements and be regular names on the scoresheet, often near the top end.

MX1 looked to be another Pichon benefit with the Honda man quickest in both free-practice outings. The 'Rocket' was also leading the way in timed practice with Ramon and Everts for close company. Pushing for a last flying lap in the dying minutes (a sometimes puzzling obsession that would prove to be costly within the upcoming rounds) Pichon stalled the Honda through a deep and slow rut, wrecking his attempt for pole number three and allowing Ramon to creep in with an effort only two-tenths faster. The Suzukis weren't faring so well on the Portuguese inclines and both Strijbos and the physically improving Smets were

Townley once again. A mature ride in Portugal netted 'BT' his second overall triumph of the year.

some distance away during free practice. Things improved marginally with a top-ten slot for both in the chrono but it was hard to see Strijbos being the same force at the front of the pack as in the first two Grand Prix. A mere two years' full-time World Championship experience clocked by the teenager were not helping him match his rivals for lines and speed around the Agueda course. The usual suspects of Coppins, Jorgensen, Smets and co. filled the first positions, with only Melotte and Strijbos conspicuous by their absence outside the first ten. The pace was fast and errors minimal with times very tight; down to James Noble in ninth the difference was less than two seconds, which is unusual. Gundersen was fourth and gave the clearest sign yet that the young KTM duo might be edging towards a possible victory.

In the Saturday afternoon press conferences there was an air of indifference towards the track. Both Pichon and Everts hoped that there would be further work undertaken to clean the deep single line through a large percentage of the circuit, otherwise acknowledging that the motos would become processional and decent starts a precious commodity. This view was more or less shared across the board but with the sun dipping out of sight the diggers began their work.

Sunday

A hefty crash at the start of the first MX1 moto ruled out the chances of a third consecutive podium for Josh Coppins. The Kiwi had his front wheel clipped by Gundersen as the KTM veered across the track on the exit of a sharp left corner and tumbled into a heap, with Smets taking severe evasive action. Coppins would clamber back on the Honda and mount a determined charge back from last to tenth position before the bike exhaled its final breath a despairing two laps from the finish. The impact of the fall had ruptured the fuel line and the 450 rolled to a halt after thirty-five hard minutes for the crestfallen twenty-seven-year-old. 'Someone hit the bike and nudged the fuel tank, because I rode my balls off to get back up to tenth and then it stopped with a lap to go. I'm disappointed but you have to accept these things,' he stoically admitted. Everts meanwhile had taken the holeshot and pulled away from Gundersen as Pichon built up his speed to also pass the Norwegian after five laps. The Grand Prix was very much between the two. Everts held the upper hand on a significantly drier and improved terrain courtesy of his superb start in the first moto. Pichon continually tried to reduce the gap and seemed to be successful thanks to the swarms of backmarkers that made life difficult for Everts and had the Yamaha man seething about the hold-up in the post-race interview. Pichon, despite a few wobbles, narrowed the margin to just 1.6 seconds in an exciting finale with further promise for more thrills later in the afternoon. Gundersen and Ramon realised their potential with subsequent positions, but Ramon was gifted fourth one lap before the finish thanks to a fall by Smets, who dropped out of the top ten. The

At last! Stephen Sword realises a dream and wins a GP moto with a resolute display of strength and concentration.

Suzuki man started brightly in Moto2 and was holding second place to Pichon, who had decided that the only way to win was to get out in front of Everts as soon as physically possible. The game plan worked as Everts lost fractions of seconds for two laps behind Smets. The hulking Belgian saw the Suzuki fade

Coppins goes down after being hit by Gundersen (10). Smets has to lose time avoiding the carnage.

Top: Townley, Sword and de Reuver on the podium.
Bottom: Pichon has time for a smile and joke with Everts in the post-race press conference.

and stall at the start of lap three and then a nasty smash casing a double on the same circulation spelt the end of his race. The handlebar dug into Smets' lower stomach and he pulled into the pits. Meanwhile Pichon cranked up the speed as much as he could until a lead of almost twenty seconds had been constructed over his rival. The matched moto scores would give Pichon the victory thanks to the second-race ranking. Everts, by now a leading world authority on the maxim of a championship being a 'marathon, not a sprint', held back in a reserved second place and had to watch the red Honda scoop its first win of the year and a debut GP triumph for the 450R. Sporting a line of hand blisters and calluses from his first-race endeavours, Coppins vented some of his frustrations with third place. Cedric Melotte thoroughly earned his second overall podium in three races and demonstrated some of the speed that earned his Zolder trophy with a steady ride in the second moto. Ken de Dijcker again was hunting positions where he

really had no right to be on the Sarholz Honda and his fifth spot in the second race would be a season high. Gundersen and Ramon had their own troubles later in the day that wrecked chances of a top-three finish. The former ran wide while trying to overtake de Dijcker and whacked a fence post with his hand, losing five places. Ramon stalled the 450 on the first lap and spent the race on a twenty-one-position-trawl through the field; the end result of which was a final overall points tally just behind Melotte.

Suzuki were rubbing their chins after a tough meeting for the Belgian crew. Some time testing and tweaking of the new 4-stroke was needed while suspicion of a rear brake problem was one possible clue towards sudden seizures of the bike. Pichon, meanwhile, was basking in the fortune reversal after Bellpuig and the end of eight months of recovery and rehabilitation to confirm that his career was again in the ascendancy. 'It seems like I have been through a very long and bad period but I never gave up and was always thinking about the time I could come back to be on top of the podium,' he said. 'I pushed hard today and I am so happy to win. I have to thank the doctors for getting me back on my feet so quickly and my team who have worked so hard and kept believing in me when our start to the season was not so good. In the second race I tried really hard to get a lead and when it was up to eighteen seconds I eased off and really enjoyed the last two laps.'

A cold first MX2 race of the day culminated in a straightforward Ben Townley victory. 'BT' was leading by halfway round the opening lap. The interest came from the dice between Sword and de Reuver for second position. Both riders were leaving nothing in the locker and the KTM pilot was the first to crack, making a mistake on lap six that let the Scotsman through to sample Townley's slowly evaporating roost first hand. Four laps later and it was once again an orange one-two with de Reuver this time able to eke away from Sword, who was tensing up, and at a late stage wisely backed off with the second moto in mind. Sword came out of the gate like a lion in the second race, claiming the holeshot and unveiling a forty-minute torrent of faultless riding that eventually broke the resilience of the chasing Townley who could not get close enough. In fairness to the Moto1 winner he rallied until the final laps but sensibly saw that the 'overall' was within sight. De Reuver hadn't made a good enough jump from the line to be vying for contention but his third place, after passing a fading Italian double of Chiodi and Cairoli, secured another podium. Sword crossed the line with his head tilted back and his fists gripped in a posture of elation and relief. It had been a long time coming for the British number one and his growing band of admirers swamped the friendly twenty-four-year-old as he prepared for his third consecutive podium ceremony. Even though more glories were to come, Sword produced his most convincing Grand Prix of the year in Portugal. After his first ever '25 points' his name was realistically accepted as a title candidate and Townley graciously acknowledged that the Kawasaki man was just too quick. The pair tied for points in the standings and it seemed that an interesting duel was forming for early season supremacy, with other players such as Rattray, McFarlane and de Reuver still to show their hand. Another highlight of the moto for British fans was the comeback by Dobb who 'shed the years' to come back from sixteenth on the first lap to fifth by the race end. Tyla Rattray was reduced to a bystander compared to the action-packed role he played in Spain. By his own downcast admission after the races he could have ridden better, but his twenty-fifth position in the gate thanks to Saturday's shambles did not help

Pichon cranked over, guiding the Honda. Portugal would give the Frenchman his first win in eleven months.

matters. Luckily for 'Styla' it would be one of the worst days of the season and easily forgettable compared to some of the results that lay ahead. Andrew McFarlane was another whose GP was determined by a mistake on Saturday and subsequent poor gate position. Better things were expected of the Australian as part of the Yamaha UK squad, especially with factory engines prepared by the Rinaldi brothers. Spanish Moto2 winner Mickael Maschio was slightly crash happy in Agueda. Falling twice in the first race and then sustaining a mild concussion in the second outing as well as damaging the front end of his bike, the Frenchman was swiftly denting his chances of challenging for the 2004 crown with some erratic displays.

There seemed to be a collective exhalation early on Sunday evening. The World Championships would now head back to northern Europe after a much-needed two-week pause.

MX1

Overall Position	No.	Rider	Nat.	Bike	Race 1 Pos (Pts)	Race 2 Pos (Pts)	Total
1	2	Pichon, Mickael	FRA	Honda	2 (22)	1 (25)	47
2	72	Everts, Stefan	BEL	Yamaha	1 (25)	2 (22)	47
3	7	Melotte, Cedric	BEL	Yamaha	5 (16)	4 (18)	34
4	11	Ramon, Steve	BEL	KTM	4 (18)	6 (15)	33
5	10	Gundersen, Kenneth	NOR	KTM	3 (20)	9 (12)	32
6	24	Strijbos, Kevin	BEL	Suzuki	6 (15)	8 (13)	28
7	27	Atsuta, Yoshitaka	JPN	Honda	12 (9)	7 (14)	23
8	6	Garcia Vico, Francisco	SPA	Honda	9 (12)	10 (11)	23
9	31	Coppins, Joshua	NZL	Honda	0	3 (20)	20
10	80	de Dijcker, Ken	BEL	Honda	0	5 (16)	16
11	26	Pyrhonen, Antti	FIN	Suzuki	14 (7)	13 (8)	15
12	53	Cooper, Paul	GBR	Honda	7 (14)	0	14
13	8	Jorgensen, Brian	DEN	Honda	10 (11)	19 (2)	13
14	48	Burnham, Christian	GBR	KTM	8 (13)	0	13
15	34	Noble, James	GBR	Honda	19 (2)	11 (10)	12
16	40	Leok, Tanel	EST	Suzuki	18 (3)	12 (9)	12
17	45	Martin, Christophe	FRA	Yamaha	17 (4)	14 (7)	11
18	74	Freibergs, Lauris	LAT	Honda	13 (8)	18 (3)	11
19	3	Smets, Joel	BEL	Suzuki	11 (10)	0	10
20	12	Theybers, Danny	BEL	Yamaha	16 (5)	17 (4)	9
21	77	Kovalainen, Marko	FIN	Honda	0	15 (6)	6
22	75	Dobes, Josef	CZE	Suzuki	20 (1)	16 (5)	6
23	18	Bervoets, Marnicq	BEL	Yamaha	15 (6)	0	6
24	50	Hucklebridge, Mark	GBR	KTM	0	20 (1)	1
25	73	Traversini, Thomas	ITA	Honda	0	0	0
26	61	Kragelj, Saso	SLO	Yamaha	0	0	0
27	216	Nambotin, Christophe	FRA	Yamaha	0	0	0
28	123	Oddenino, Enrico	ITA	TM	0	0	0
29	215	Santos, Hugo	POR	Honda	0	0	0
30	43	Meo, Antoine	FRA	Kawasaki	0	0	0
31	85	Turpin, Vincent	FRA	Honda	0	0	0

MX1 World Championship standings:

Everts 129, Melotte 103, Ramon 102, Coppins 98, Gundersen 93, Pichon 91, Strijbos 68, Garcia Vico 65, Smets 62, Jorgensen 60, Leok 57, Noble 47, de Dijcker 45, Cooper 42, Atsuta 37, Bervoets 32, Pyrhonen 31, Freibergs 29, Burnham 27, Martin 25, Theybers 24, Kovalainen 17, Hucklebridge 15, Dobes 8, Breugelmans 7, Turpin 5, Meo 4, Dini 3.

MX2

Overall Position	No.	Rider	Nat.	Bike	Race 1 Pos (Pts)	Race 2 Pos (Pts)	Total
1	30	Townley, Ben	NZL	KTM	1 (25)	2 (22)	47
2	19	Sword, Stephen	GBR	Kawasaki	3 (20)	1 (25)	45
3	17	de Reuver, Marc	NED	KTM	2 (22)	3 (20)	42
4	55	Nunn, Carl	GBR	Honda	7 (14)	7 (14)	28
5	222	Cairoli, Antonio	ITA	Yamaha	12 (9)	4 (18)	27
6	16	Rattray, Tyla	RSA	KTM	6 (15)	10 (11)	26
7	15	McFarlane, Andrew	AUS	Yamaha	4 (18)	14 (7)	25
8	64	Dobb, James	GBR	Honda	15 (6)	5 (16)	22
9	4	Chiodi, Alessio	ITA	Yamaha	13 (8)	8 (13)	21
10	52	Leuret, Pascal	FRA	KTM	8 (13)	15 (6)	19
11	68	Philippaerts, David	ITA	KTM	9 (12)	17 (4)	16
12	90	Pourcel, Sebastien	FRA	Kawasaki	5 (16)	0	16
13	5	Bartolini, Andrea	ITA	Yamaha	0	6 (15)	15
14	56	Priem, Manuel	BEL	Suzuki	17 (4)	11 (10)	14
15	76	Leok, Aigar	EST	KTM	16 (5)	12 (9)	14
16	38	van Daele, Marvin	BEL	Suzuki	0	9 (12)	12
17	211	Mackenzie, Billy	GBR	Yamaha	10 (11)	0	11
18	118	Boissiere, Anthony	FRA	Yamaha	19 (2)	13 (8)	10
19	71	Maschio, Mickael	FRA	Kawasaki	11 (10)	0	10
20	87	Dement, Jeff	USA	Honda	18 (3)	16 (5)	8
21	66	Stevanini, Christian	ITA	Honda	14 (7)	0	7
22	65	Monni, Manuel	ITA	Yamaha	0	18 (3)	3
23	114	Swanepoel, Garreth	RSA	KTM	0	19 (2)	2
24	83	Barragan, Jonathan	SPA	KTM	0	20 (1)	1
25	70	Church, Tom	GBR	Kawasaki	20 (1)	0	1
26	92	Cherubini, Luca	ITA	Suzuki	0	0	0
27	46	Guarnieri, Davide	ITA	KTM	0	0	0
28	49	Goncalves, Rui	POR	Yamaha	0	0	0
29	202	Smith, Wayne	GBR	KTM	0	0	0
30	37	Caps, Patrick	BEL	Yamaha	0	0	0

MX2 World Championship standings:

Townley 119, Sword 119, de Reuver 103, McFarlane 98, Rattray 83, Leok 75, Dobb 71, Maschio 67, Nunn 56, Cairoli 55, Philippaerts 43, Priem 42, Pourcel 39, Boissiere 38, van Daele 36, Barragan 35, Leuret 32, Bartolini 24, Church 24, Cepelak 22, Chiodi 21, Mackenzie 19, Dement 18, Goncalves 16, Monni 16, Federici 13, Swanepoel 11, Stevanini 7, Letellier 6, Avis 5, Cherubini 5, Barreda 3, Caps 2, Bernardez 2, Smith 1.

round four
Grand Prix of the Netherlands
Valkenswaard, 24-25 April 2004

The MX2 qualifying heats were predictably a Townley-de Reuver affair. The Kiwi held off a strong challenge from Stephen Sword in the first race after Tyla Rattray had somehow managed to take the holeshot going through the fast right-left kink at the end of the lengthy start straight. One of the quickest and visually stunning sections in Grand Prix motocross, watching the riders flick right and then skim the waist-high grassy ledge as they lean left to hit the first jump is quite breathtaking, especially considering the surface and the constant weaving instability of the motorcycle as it struggles for traction. Townley swept across the finish line just over a second in front of Sword for another pole position as Portuguese Yamaha rider Rui Concalves claimed what would be his best qualification of the season in fourth behind Rattray. At the start of the second heat Jamie Dobb's afternoon was cut short before he had time to dive into the curves with the rest of the pack as Christian Stevanini fell behind him. Somehow the Italian got his arm caught

Above: Andrea Bartolini and Wyatt Avis on the grooved and weaving sandy terrain.
Opposite Page: Sword, hounded by Rattray, is unable to make the podium for the first time in 2004.

in the rear wheel of the Briton's Honda. Dragged like a doll for ten yards before the mangled mess of man and machine came to a halt, Stevanini was taken to hospital with lacerations and a dislocation. Mickael Maschio also crashed at the same point and so began another underwhelming weekend for the Frenchman. De Reuver took some time to regain his composure after his ostrich impression in the morning and took the majority of the race to pass Cairoli, who was growing in stature and reputation with every Grand Prix. Mickael Pichon produced what he described as the 'perfect lap' in the MX1 Timed Practice to cast aside the speed and effort clocked by former Suzuki teammate and protégé Kevin Strijbos, who had been topping the timing screens for a large chunk of the period. Strijbos had scored his best ever GP result at Valkenswaard with fourth place in 2003, riding the Suzuki RM250 in only his second full season of World Championship racing. The teenager had become a pleasant and vital addition to the paddock. Like most of his age group Strijbos seemed to be physically expanding over the passing months and his awareness of what was required to lead and win motos was growing in kind. Strijbos was testing his mettle against the world's best, having moved straight to the premier class from a single sporadic season in the 125s in 2001 and was now in his first campaign on a 450. His rate of improvement was easily visible and he became one of the truly thrilling prospects for the future of World Championship motocross. His riding style revealed ease and determination with a dose of rough edges. Kevin is painfully shy but is very easy to make laugh, which is an endearing characteristic as a smile is never far away.

Kenneth Gundersen, who has a fine pedigree riding in the sand thanks to his Champ KTM apprenticeship in 2000 and 2001, was third-quickest, placing in the top three in both free practice sessions and seemingly a decent bet for podium contention on Sunday. Stefan Everts was fourth in front of Melotte with the top five separated by a second and a half; although Pichon was over a second faster than Strijbos. Six Belgian riders littered the top eight as de Dijcker, Ramon and Smets also filled the leaderboard. Coppins was ninth in front of Antti Pyrhonen who was having a hard time living with the Suzuki 250 in a fleet of 4-strokes.

Sunday

From top of the podium one week to missing out altogether the next, Valkenswaard was to be the last low point for Pichon in terms of his results being affected by his own hand. The day was one of celebration for the L&M Yamaha squad as Melotte and Everts were victorious in both races, ending with the same

Josh Coppins has good reason to ponder after a bad weekend in Holland. It would soon get much better for the Kiwi.

overall points tally but Everts picking up the GP winner's trophy because of his strong second moto performance once again. Stefan was now out of the blocks for his eighth world title after recovering from the rib and hand injuries.

The first race was a runaway win for Melotte, who quickly moved to pass holeshotter Ramon and built up a lead of some thirteen seconds over the chasing hordes. A tussle for second erupted between Everts, Strijbos, Pichon, Ramon and Smets, with de Dijcker keeping a detached presence. Ramon tumbled off on lap four and would spend the rest of the moto in sixth place before being humbled by de Dijcker. Strijbos and Smets circulated in tandem adrift of Melotte for four laps before Everts picked up his pace from fourth and overtook both of his countrymen to cross the chequered flag second. Like Ramon, Pichon also hit the ground. He had been following Everts closely when he lost the front end of the Honda coming into the fast right corner that led into two large jumps down to the pits and finish. He later claimed that he did not know why the bike suddenly washed-out but it was possible that Everts had flicked up some stones that left the front Pirelli hungry for grip. It had not been a good outing for fellow Honda rider Josh Coppins. As the Kiwi went over the steep first jump on the course

mid-pack starting the second lap he also went over the bars, vanishing from sight in an almost comical image. A result of pushing too hard after a mediocre start, Coppins would overcook his efforts again and fall a second time, on this occasion damaging the bike and his right hand, necessitating a long visit to the pits. It would be his worst moto of 2004 and although a fifth position in the second race reclaimed a few points Coppins was seeing his positive start to the year begin to tail-off. Smets was able to enjoy his first decent moto finish on the better-behaved Suzuki as Pichon recovered enough composure to just pip Strijbos to fourth.

The Frenchman began the second moto with better intentions, leading the first five laps, but was not riding in the same league as the Yamaha duo, who were more in tune with the circuit. Melotte surged to the front again but Everts had learned his teammate's ploy from earlier in the day and quickly chased through to second, biding his time until the pace slowed and he was able to push ahead, maintaining his consistency. Pichon, prone to more errors than usual, saw tenths disappear from his lap times as Smets, who had completed the first lap in the top three, relegated the Honda to make the podium an all-Belgian affair (unsurprisingly). Strijbos could not live with the speed of the leaders.

After the win Everts alluded to the feelings of exhaustion echoed by Strijbos and Pichon. 'I was very close to my maximum speed in the second moto but I knew that I had to stay with Cedric because he would tire. In the championship everything is going according to plan for me but I know it will be a long and hard season. Getting some rest in between GPs will be crucial.' Smets, on the other hand, was taking all the races he could find after missing a wealth of development and race time with the Suzuki. 'After ten years with a European bike the Suzuki was a complete new engine and chassis and I put a lot of pressure on myself since last October to make this project work. Mantova was a huge setback but now I am following the plan exactly how I wanted after discussing it with my doctors. I was aiming for top eight in Zolder, top five in Spain and then podium and victory at Portugal through to this GP. The goal is to keep on improving my speed and results.' Sadly for Smets this would be the bright spot of a personally difficult 2004. The ex-KTM stalwart faced an arduous campaign ahead with his knee but other outside factors would soon rob the paddock of his presence.

Ben Townley was able to crack open champagne bottle number three of the season in the MX2 class, but it was a close call. 'T-dog', as was now etched on his pit board by mechanic Craig, crashed on the fifth lap of the first moto after passing lightning-starter Cairoli for the lead. It was a cautionary slip and number 30 lost only three positions and five laps before he was again able to

Above: Mickael Pichon finally comes to rest after a fast practice get-off.
Left: Kenneth Gundersen is caught out by the tight chicane near the finish line.

see a clear track ahead of him. In the meantime Cairoli held off a strong assault from de Reuver who then began to slow and was spitting mad as the KTM again didn't fancy the long haul. Townley glided past Rattray (whose new 125cc engine assisted enormously in pulling free of his pursuers) before swooping on Cairoli, who lasted the distance in the top three but was a country mile behind the KTMs. Sword just defeated a wounded McFarlane in a tight finish. Claudio Federici classified with his highest position yet despite a foot injury, and for once was showing signs of not accepting the minor humiliation by his rookie teammate Cairoli. De Reuver was not to be placated in the second moto. A problematic gearbox locked the KTM into fifth during the final three laps and dropped him down to fourth. Up until the moment of frustration the two 250 riders had been having a very watchable fight for the lead, with numerous line changes and a nice game of cat-and-mouse happening between perennial leader Townley and

the Dutchman looking to satisfy his supporters. Rattray kept in contact and was ready to assume the runner-up spot as de Reuver lost speed. Alessio Chiodi also benefited from his refusal to concede to the KTM onslaught and pushed to claim third from de Reuver on the last lap. The Italian would mount the podium surprised at his speed after recent hand treatment. Sword missed out on his fourth trophy by a single point but confessed that he rode most of the second moto 'out of control'. During the first race he suffered with some rear brake fade that would be the first little sign that the Kawasaki was not as bulletproof as everyone thought. His fourth place overall was still his best ever result at Valkenswaard. Carl Nunn was fifth in Moto2 and would look back at the Dutch Grand Prix as his highest race finish.

The first 'double' of the year in the MX2 class gave Townley a seventeen-point gap over Sword in the standings. McFarlane's resilience also kept the Australian in the hunt. Pichon held fourth in the MX1 series after not being able to extend his Portuguese form; he left the paddock forty-nine points behind Everts but would only have to wait six days before having another crack.

motocross
2004 Grand Prix Review

MX1

Overall Position	No.	Rider	Nat.	Bike	Race 1 Pos (Pts)	Race 2 Pos (Pts)	Total
1	72	Everts, Stefan	BEL	Yamaha	2 (22)	1 (25)	47
2	7	Melotte, Cedric	BEL	Yamaha	1 (25)	2 (22)	47
3	3	Smets, Joel	BEL	Suzuki	3 (20)	3 (20)	40
4	2	Pichon, Mickael	FRA	Honda	4 (18)	4 (18)	36
5	24	Strijbos, Kevin	BEL	Suzuki	5 (16)	6 (15)	31
6	10	Gundersen, Kenneth	NOR	KTM	8 (13)	7 (14)	27
7	11	Ramon, Steve	BEL	KTM	7 (14)	8 (13)	27
8	80	de Dijcker, Ken	BEL	Honda	6 (15)	9 (12)	27
9	27	Atsuta, Yoshitaka	JPN	Honda	11 (10)	11 (10)	20
10	74	Freibergs, Lauris	LAT	Honda	14 (7)	10 (11)	18
11	40	Leok, Tanel	EST	Suzuki	13 (8)	12 (9)	17
12	31	Coppins, Joshua	NZL	Honda	0	5 (16)	16
13	12	Theybers, Danny	BEL	Yamaha	12 (9)	14 (7)	16
14	77	Kovalainen, Marko	FIN	Honda	16 (5)	13 (8)	13
15	48	Burnham, Christian	GBR	KTM	9 (12)	0	12
16	18	Bervoets, Marnicq	BEL	Yamaha	10 (11)	0	11
17	50	Hucklebridge, Mark	GBR	KTM	18 (3)	15 (6)	9
18	26	Pyrhonen, Antti	FIN	Suzuki	15 (6)	18 (3)	9
19	28	Seguy, Luigi	FRA	Yamaha	19 (2)	16 (5)	7
20	45	Martin, Christophe	FRA	Yamaha	17 (4)	19 (2)	6
21	73	Traversini, Thomas	ITA	Honda	0	17 (4)	4
22	101	Robins, Erwin	NED	Yamaha	0	20 (1)	1
23	411	Verhoeven, Bas	NED	Honda	20 (1)	0	1
24	123	Oddenino, Enrico	ITA	TM	0	0	0
25	36	Flockhart, Stuart	GBR	Honda	0	0	0
26	221	van den Berg, Heikki	NED	Yamaha	0	0	0
27	208	Boekhorst, Gert Jan	NED	KTM	0	0	0
28	6	Garcia Vico, Francisco	SPA	Honda	0	0	0
29	220	Das, Michael	NED	Honda	0	0	0
30	43	Meo, Antoine	FRA	Kawasaki	0	0	0
31	75	Dobes, Josef	CZE	Suzuki	0	0	0

MX1 World Championship standings:

Everts 176, Melotte 150, Ramon 129, Pichon 127, Gundersen 120, Coppins 114, Smets 102, Strijbos 99, Leok 74, de Dijcker 72, Garcia Vico 65, Jorgensen 60, Atsuta 57, Noble 47, Freibergs 47, Bervoets 43, Cooper 42, Theybers 40, Pyrhonen 40, Burnham 39, Martin 31, Kovalainen 30, Hucklebridge 24, Dobes 8, Seguy 7, Breugelmans 7, Turpin 5, Traversini 4, Meo 4, Dini 3, Robins 1, Verhoeven 1.

MX2

Overall Position	No.	Rider	Nat.	Bike	Race 1 Pos (Pts)	Race 2 Pos (Pts)	Total
1	30	Townley, Ben	NZL	KTM	1 (25)	1 (25)	50
2	16	Rattray, Tyla	RSA	KTM	2 (22)	2 (22)	44
3	4	Chiodi, Alessio	ITA	Yamaha	7 (14)	3 (20)	34
4	19	Sword, Stephen	GBR	Kawasaki	4 (18)	6 (15)	33
5	222	Cairoli, Antonio	ITA	Yamaha	3 (20)	10 (11)	31
6	15	McFarlane, Andrew	AUS	Yamaha	5 (16)	7 (14)	30
7	55	Nunn, Carl	GBR	Honda	9 (12)	5 (16)	28
8	22	Federici, Claudio	ITA	Yamaha	6 (15)	9 (12)	27
9	17	de Reuver, Marc	NED	KTM	0	4 (18)	18
10	68	Philippaerts, David	ITA	KTM	13 (8)	11 (10)	18
11	5	Bartolini, Andrea	ITA	Yamaha	11 (10)	14 (7)	17
12	211	Mackenzie, Billy	GBR	Yamaha	20 (1)	8 (13)	14
13	114	Swanepoel, Garreth	RSA	KTM	12 (9)	17 (4)	13
14	71	Maschio, Mickael	FRA	Kawasaki	8 (13)	0	13
15	87	Dement, Jeff	USA	Honda	15 (6)	15 (6)	12
16	83	Barragan, Jonathan	SPA	KTM	10 (11)	0	11
17	49	Goncalves, Rui	POR	Yamaha	0	12 (9)	9
18	90	Pourcel, Sebastien	FRA	Kawasaki	0	13 (8)	8
19	64	Dobb, James	GBR	Honda	14 (7)	0	7
20	76	Leok, Aigar	EST	KTM	0	16 (5)	5
21	37	Caps, Patrick	BEL	Yamaha	16 (5)	0	5
22	92	Cherubini, Luca	ITA	Suzuki	17 (4)	0	4
23	95	Nagl, Maximilian	GER	KTM	0	18 (3)	3
24	202	Smith, Wayne	GBR	KTM	18 (3)	0	3
25	70	Church, Tom	GBR	Kawasaki	0	19 (2)	2
26	121	Salaets, Kristof	BEL	Honda	19 (2)	0	2
27	99	Vromans, Oscar	NED	Yamaha	0	20 (1)	1
28	38	van Daele, Marvin	BEL	Suzuki	0	0	0
29	207	Seronval, Steve	BEL	Honda	0	0	0
30	227	Strik, George	NED	KTM	0	0	0

MX2 World Championship standings:

Townley 169, Sword 152, McFarlane 128, Rattray 127, de Reuver 121, Cairoli 86, Nunn 84, Maschio 80, Leok 80, Dobb 78, Philippaerts 61, Chiodi 55, Pourcel 47, Barragan 46, Priem 42, Bartolini 41, Federici 40, Boissiere 38, van Daele 36, Mackenzie 33, Leuret 32, Dement 30, Church 26, Goncalves 25, Swanepoel 24, Cepelak 22, Monni 16, Cherubini 9, Stevanini 7, Caps 7, Letellier 6, Avis 5, Smith 4, Nagl 3, Barreda 3, Bernardez 2, Salaets 2, Vromans 1.

Pichon grimaces his way through the motos on Sunday after a high-speed scare during qualification.

Grand Prix of Germany
Teutschenthal, 1-2 May 2004

Thankfully the grins on the podium were bigger than the medical centre's logbook list, and both were sizeable entities. Round five of the World Championship, the German Grand Prix at the rural Talkessel circuit, was a stand-out race for both positive and negative reasons. Stephen Sword and Brian Jorgensen were deserved and refreshing debut winners in each class but the weekend was overshadowed by several accidents that sent a wave of alarm and concern across the paddock.

The MX Grand Prix circus had slow-steamed from Holland across Germany to the opposite border, and the quaint setting of Teutschenthal, just outside the former Eastern Bloc city of Leipzig. Talkessel is spectacularly submerged in the rolling fields outside of the confused metropolis that still bears so many marks of the country's recent ragged history in the easily recognisable contrast of economic aesthetic. The bright golden meadows surrounding the venue verged on postcard beauty. Teutschenthal is always a large draw for fans thanks to its isolated nature and the raucous evening entertainment supplied by the club. Joel Smets famously gave an irate press conference twelve months ago, sitting next to then-KTM teammate and the somewhat bemused Pit Beirer, threatening to burn down the adjacent beer tent for the sheer amount of racket that was echoing around the facility and penetrating the living area. While the unusually enormous bouncers/security guards kept their eyes peeled for a six-foot blond Belgian with a gas can in tow this time, Smets wisely decided to avoid any chance of a lack of sleep by camping in the nearby hamlet of Teutschenthal village; apparently much happier for his escape. Talkessel was like Valkenswaard in its historical relevance

to motocross. It had hosted GP events for over thirty years and even for both East and West Germany before the unification. The track itself was largely 'untouched' and was close to being something of a relic in terms of modern Grand Prix circuits. Riders both loved and feared Teutschenthal. Undulating and grippy, with deep cambered turns, high jumps and a flowing layout; Talkessel was a tour de force of off-road motorcycle riding. It was, however, also the fastest track on the calendar and this elevated the level of danger in an already hazardous occupation. There was an admiration and sense of caution and respect when the riders talked about Teutschenthal. There were no whoops, doubles or triples, switchbacks, chicanes or rhythm sections, just a flat-out chance to race and ride motorcycles to a physical limit. The common feeling towards the track was that it would be an excellent place to train and practice but racing was another matter.

The crashes that knocked out both Andrea Bartolini and Mickael Pichon and wrecked the seasons of Marc de Reuver, Kenneth Gundersen and Billy Mackenzie were serious incidents that could have been a lot worse. The medical attention and provisions were good but couldn't disguise the notion that Talkessel was simply 'out of date' and too quick for the modern motocross machine.

Ben Townley arrived and left Germany in very different states of mind. Walking around the paddock on a high after his double win at Valkenswaard in spite of ankle pain, he would be driving through the gates back to the airport a confused and frustrated young man on Sunday evening. He also had the off-track distraction of his KTM contract that was due to expire at the end of the season. BT had committed to another year in Europe and publicly declared he would be moving to MX1 for 2005, which instigated a busy time for his manager, with Suzuki very interested in acquiring his services. The hottest young rider was on the market and his stock was rising at every GP; to draw correlations to his mysterious second-moto lack of concentration and crash was not terribly difficult.

The racing was eventful and exciting for its moments of drama and posterity rather than gripping because of the riding skills on display. The low grey clouds on Sunday once more successfully read the mood of the paddock and it is safe to say that while many riders may have been looking forward to the Grand Prix at Teutschenthal, a bigger percentage were glad to leave it behind; except for Stephen Sword and Brian Jorgensen...

Saturday

MX1 Timed Practice was held in two rather disorganised parts after Mickael Pichon's horrifying crash at high speed and the subsequent red flag sliced the last minutes from the initial session. Riders were recalled after the track was cleared but apparently not everyone knew about the continuance, assuming that the lap times would be taken from the moment the period was curtailed. The exercise was pointless as nobody significantly improved their ranking and Pichon had his fourth pole from five GPs with the same effort he had recorded prior to taking a heavy risk to go even faster. The accident was seen as needless in many eyes and puzzled the majority, particularly Pichon's teammate, the returning Brian Jorgensen, who ended up third in the gate and was pushing for pole position. On only his third lap of seven Pichon had registered a time that was 1.2 seconds ahead of the rest as Kevin Strijbos again proved to be up to the task in qualification. Only one second divided Strijbos in second down to his teammate Smets in ninth with Pichon once more in his own zone. The reasons for another flying lap remain a mystery but the consequences ultimately cost the Honda rider serious ground in the World Championship. The first downhill right turn after the start drives down into a steep bomb hole with a fast approach up into a flat thirty-yard run to the finish line table top; an intimidating jump due to its size and speed on the entry. Pichon streaked through the downhill dip and changed line to avoid a slower rider on the uphill approach, hitting a bump in doing so and pitching the Honda onto the front wheel in a reverse wheelie for the flat stretch before the table top. Unable to bail out because of the bike's inverted position at such rapid force the 450 eventually buckled and chucked its rider into the face of the jump. Pichon was knocked out and could not feel his legs when he groggily came around. People flooded the track as the session was immediately stopped and the irony of Pit Beirer's presence at his home GP, after a big accident at the Bulgarian round in 2003 left the German star paralysed, was not lost on the concerned multitude for a worrying thirty minutes. After what seemed like an age, Pichon was released and he eased away from the medical centre having sustained a hard impact to the neck and shoulders. The assumption was naturally made that he was out for the races but this was surprisingly rebuked late on Saturday evening when the team announced that the twenty-eight-year-old would attempt the warm-up and try for some points.

Townley provided a small preview of what would come to pass during Sunday's races when he slipped off while leading the first MX2 qualifying heat and finished fourth, letting Mickael Maschio enjoy pole-position status on a weekend when the Kawasakis were looking particularly sturdy. Also riding a green 250, Sebastien Pourcel was in good form and wrestling the 4-stroke around the German curves in an eye-pleasingly liberal style. His second position would be one of his best heat performances of the year, but over-exuberance matched with a lack of experience ruled out an overall Grand Prix result on Sunday that his talent merited. By the time the World Championships visited Germany for a second time later in the season the French teenager had learned his lesson to positive effect. An Italian Yamaha again led the MX2 field in the second qualifying sprint but this time a '2' digit was missing from the plate. An identical figure in livery and colour to his De Carli teammate Cairoli (222), Claudio Federici (22), was out in front from start to finish as Sword and de Reuver slowly caught up. Cairoli was sixth.

Sunday

The 'Pichon table top' became a hot spot for controversy on a damp and colder Sunday programme of races. The rider himself managed seven laps of warm-up thanks to painkilling injections in both shoulders and gained many admirers for his bravery by taking to the gate and salvaging twenty-three points with top-ten finishes in both motos. 'During the motos I was OK until about ten minutes into the race, and then had no strength in my upper body,' he winced afterwards.

'Ups and downs'. Teutschenthal is one of the most spectacular tracks on the schedule but it is also one of the fastest.

'With this condition I am happy with tenth and ninth. Now I must see my specialist and rest before Lichtenvoorde.'

The other victims were Bartolini and de Reuver. The Italian went down in the final two laps of the first moto in a carbon-copy of the Pichon crash but was concussed and suffered internal bleeding. The race was stopped as the stretchers were again unfolded. The former 1999 500cc World Champion is an immensely popular figure in Grand Prix motocross. His accident and condition again had many paddock personnel ashen-faced for the lengthy duration it took for word to establish that the Yamaha rider was okay. Weeping with the scare and in shock, it is fair to say that the German crash (in a season generally littered with small injury hiccups) helped contribute to Andrea's decision to end a successful career at the final Grand Prix of the year. De Reuver's fall unbelievably occurred at the same location but had more terrifying potential as he clipped another rider lining up the table top during the first twenty seconds of the second moto. The Dutchman had already retired in the opening event with yet more mechanical trouble. Hitting the ground in the middle of the pack he was lucky not to be struck and onlookers at the section were by now very understandably jumpy about any further incident. Fortunately de Reuver was able to walk away immediately but an X-ray and examination several days afterwards on a painful back revealed fractured vertebrae, and the necessary operation effectively ended the KTM rider's title ambitions. In the same race Billy Mackenzie detached from his Yamaha at the highest peak of the big jump adjacent to the pits and broke his collarbone, as well as hurting his back and several ribs. It was a monumental 'get-off', and visible from everywhere at the circuit thanks to the sheer height achieved by spiralling rider and bike. The accident was caused by the twenty-year-old's inability to brake on the approach to the jump due to the pedal clogging with mud. It would be the first wake-up call for the highly rated British youngster who has a tendency to let his desire to win get ahead of him.

The day began accordingly when Pourcel fell on the first corner and Rattray crashed running over him; the South African would continue his alternating pattern of podium appearances with seventh position overall. Patrick Caps then touched McFarlane shortly afterwards, sending the Australian onto the ground. Chiodi had holeshotted but Townley worked his way up from fourth to first place in as many laps before he then embarked on his now-customary break from his adversaries. Maschio chased down Sword in second place for three circulations in a tense Kawasaki stand-off, with the Frenchman gaining the advantage. Federici was fourth.

Above: Ben Townley recovers the fallen KTM after his mistake but the podium has already vanished.
Below: Stephen Sword rushes ahead to become the first British winner of a GP since 2002.

Above: Cedric Melotte was happy to be among the leaders again and with another podium trophy.

motocross
2004 Grand Prix Review

The fateful second race saw Chiodi again sprightly off the line but was passed quickly by Maschio. Townley forced his way ahead by the fifth lap but in the early stages of his separation a rare moment of distraction saw the championship leader lose balance on a steep downhill. A hesitant flag marshal prevented the shocked rider from being able to lift the KTM and restart without fear of being clattered by riders cresting the blind descent. In last place by some distance and probably prompted by despondency as much as the pain in his right hand, Townley coasted around the rest of the track and into the pits. The orange target may have gone but the carrot became bigger and juicier as Maschio and Sword

now both chased Grand Prix victory. Maschio was hindered by a poor tyre choice, and that helped Sword front the world for the last seven laps and break his GP duck. They crossed the finish line less than two seconds between them, with Federici's third place confirming a first MX2 top three.

Sword, now with four podiums from five, two moto wins, one overall and the red number plate as the new championship leader, was naturally ecstatic. 'This season has gone better than I could have imagined. This first win has felt like a long time coming but it is something myself and the team have worked towards. I don't feel any pressure leading the championship but I know that this title has

Below: Brian Jorgensen (8) holeshots and dominates the day with two moto victories.

to be won by consistent riding and not by making crashes and mistakes just as Townley has done.'

Brian Jorgensen, well-prepared after his operation and sufficient recovery time away from racing, rounded out the debut winner's party with two dominant motos. The amiable twenty-nine-year-old shocked everyone and perhaps even himself to a degree, judging by the humility of his post-race reaction, by holeshotting both races and setting an untouchable pace. Everts was not on form for the first moto while Pichon was just clinging onto the bike. It was left to Cedric Melotte to offer resistance to the Honda's flight once Strijbos again was victim to mechanical trouble and fell at slow speed while second, seven laps before the chequered flag. Ramon was steady but not proactive in third place and was easily passed by the Yamahas. Melotte chased Jorgensen hard in the final third of the race duration. The leader looked over his shoulder more frequently at the gaining number '7' but then found a second wind to keep a four-second cushion over his growing blue shadow.

The second moto saw Everts find his rhythm. He was held up by Gundersen in third spot for eight laps and this shredded his chances of catching Jorgensen, although the hunt throughout the latter half of the moto was entertaining fare with a tense finale as the Honda rider was able to triumph by a mere half-second. Series leader by thirty points, Everts was among the first to congratulate Jorgensen in the post-race hubbub and the high regard in which the Dane is held was noticed by the general air of good feeling towards his maiden success. Jorgensen, naturally, was over the moon. 'This is fantastic for me,' he said. 'A result in the top five today would have been good but it is an incredible feeling to win the way I did and be on top of the podium. I basically got my head down and did the job. I had some pain towards the end of the second moto but when someone like Stefan is chasing you it gives some extra energy. This is like a dream come true.'

Smets, Coppins and Melotte rounded out the top five with the Yamaha boys scaling the podium for the third GP in a row. Kenneth Gundersen finished eighth after a poor start in the first moto and should have taken fourth place in the second race, until the KTM squirmed sideways on a quick, low step-down four laps from the end and threw the Norwegian into a bundle. Crawling painfully to the side of the track, peak smashed and looking the worse for wear, the knee that Gundersen tightly held was more seriously damaged than originally thought. A broken cartilage and wrecked ligaments spelt the end of his championship. Although he would attempt to race intermittently in the next few Grand Prix

Claudio Federici finally puts young upstart teammate Cairoli behind him to earn some overdue silverware.

the super-fit twenty-two-year-old, who claimed his only premier class victory at Teutschenthal in 2002, was often left crying in pain. After the Grand Prix of Sweden the number 10 machine was no longer seen in the MX1 class with KTM bosses ordering the conscientious Gundersen away from the circuits until he felt able to compete.

The good feeling generated by the career-landmark achievements of Sword and Jorgensen helped dispel a looming shadow over the German Grand Prix, shaking up the championship standings and proving that although already five rounds old, the season was still willing to twist and turn.

motocross
2004 Grand Prix Review

MX1

Overall Position	No.	Rider	Nat.	Bike	Race 1 Pos (Pts)	Race 2 Pos (Pts)	Total
1	8	Jorgensen, Brian	DEN	Honda	1 (25)	1 (25)	50
2	72	Everts, Stefan	BEL	Yamaha	3 (20)	2 (22)	42
3	7	Melotte, Cedric	BEL	Yamaha	2 (22)	5 (16)	38
4	3	Smets, Joel	BEL	Suzuki	5 (16)	3 (20)	36
5	31	Coppins, Joshua	NZL	Honda	6 (15)	4 (18)	33
6	11	Ramon, Steve	BEL	KTM	4 (18)	6 (15)	33
7	18	Bervoets, Marnicq	BEL	Yamaha	7 (14)	7 (14)	28
8	2	Pichon, Mickael	FRA	Honda	10 (11)	9 (12)	23
9	40	Leok, Tanel	EST	Suzuki	11 (10)	10 (11)	21
10	6	Garcia Vico, Francisco	SPA	Honda	12 (9)	11 (10)	19
11	12	Theybers, Danny	BEL	Yamaha	13 (8)	13 (8)	16
12	28	Seguy, Luigi	FRA	Yamaha	14 (7)	14 (7)	14
13	24	Strijbos, Kevin	BEL	Suzuki	0	8 (13)	13
14	10	Gundersen, Kenneth	NOR	KTM	8 (13)	0	13
15	80	de Dijcker, Ken	BEL	Honda	9 (12)	0	12
16	48	Burnham, Christian	GBR	KTM	17 (4)	15 (6)	10
17	27	Atsuta, Yoshitaka	JPN	Honda	16 (5)	16 (5)	10
18	120	Dugmore, Collin	RSA	Honda	0	12 (9)	9
19	26	Pyrhonen, Antti	FIN	Suzuki	18 (3)	17 (4)	7
20	73	Traversini, Thomas	ITA	Honda	15 (6)	0	6
21	74	Freibergs, Lauris	LAT	Honda	19 (2)	18 (3)	5
22	36	Flockhart, Stuart	GBR	Honda	0	19 (2)	2
23	50	Hucklebridge, Mark	GBR	KTM	0	20 (1)	1
24	77	Kovalainen, Marko	FIN	Honda	20 (1)	0	1
25	61	Kragelj, Saso	SLO	Yamaha	0	0	0
26	123	Oddenino, Enrico	ITA	TM	0	0	0
27	231	Paasch, Sebastian	GER	Yamaha	0	0	0
28	232	Schröter, Dennis	GER	Honda	0	0	0
29	91	Dorsch, Marco	GER	Kawasaki	0	0	0
30	45	Martin, Christophe	FRA	Yamaha	0	0	0

MX1 World Championship standings:

Everts 218, Melotte 188, Ramon 162, Pichon 150, Coppins 147, Smets 138, Gundersen 133, Strijbos 112, Jorgensen 110, Leok 95, Garcia Vico 84, de Dijcker 84, Bervoets 71, Atsuta 67, Theybers 56, Freibergs 52, Burnham 49, Noble 47, Pyrhonen 47, Cooper 42, Kovalainen 31, Martin 31, Hucklebridge 25, Seguy 21, Traversini 10, Dugmore 9, Dobes 8, Breugelmans 7, Turpin 5, Meo 4, Dini 3, Flockhart 2, Robins 1, Verhoeven 1.

MX2

Overall Position	No.	Rider	Nat.	Bike	Race 1 Pos (Pts)	Race 2 Pos (Pts)	Total
1	19	Sword, Stephen	GBR	Kawasaki	3 (20)	1 (25)	45
2	71	Maschio, Mickael	FRA	Kawasaki	2 (22)	2 (22)	44
3	22	Federici, Claudio	ITA	Yamaha	4 (18)	3 (20)	38
4	37	Caps, Patrick	BEL	Yamaha	6 (15)	4 (18)	33
5	222	Cairoli, Antonio	ITA	Yamaha	8 (13)	6 (15)	28
6	64	Dobb, James	GBR	Honda	7 (14)	8 (13)	27
7	16	Rattray, Tyla	RSA	KTM	12 (9)	5 (16)	25
8	30	Townley, Ben	NZL	KTM	1 (25)	0	25
9	15	McFarlane, Andrew	AUS	Yamaha	13 (8)	7 (14)	22
10	87	Dement, Jeff	USA	Honda	11 (10)	11 (10)	20
11	52	Leuret, Pascal	FRA	KTM	14 (7)	9 (12)	19
12	4	Chiodi, Alessio	ITA	Yamaha	5 (16)	0	16
13	90	Pourcel, Sebastien	FRA	Kawasaki	15 (6)	12 (9)	15
14	76	Leok, Aigar	EST	KTM	16 (5)	13 (8)	13
15	83	Barragan, Jonathan	SPA	KTM	9 (12)	0	12
16	118	Boissiere, Anthony	FRA	Yamaha	0	10 (11)	11
17	38	van Daele, Marvin	BEL	Suzuki	10 (11)	0	11
18	95	Nagl, Maximilian	GER	KTM	17 (4)	15 (6)	10
19	55	Nunn, Carl	GBR	Honda	0	14 (7)	7
20	114	Swanepoel, Garreth	RSA	KTM	0	16 (5)	5
21	711	Allier, Tomas	FRA	Kawasaki	0	17 (4)	4
22	121	Salaets, Kristof	BEL	Honda	0	18 (3)	3
23	207	Seronval, Steve	BEL	Honda	20 (1)	19 (2)	3
24	69	Avis, Wyatt	RSA	Suzuki	18 (3)	0	3
25	201	Kulhavy, Josef	SVK	KTM	19 (2)	0	2
26	204	Campano, Carlos	SPA	Yamaha	0	20 (1)	1
27	92	Cherubini, Luca	ITA	Suzuki	0	0	0
28	211	Mackenzie, Billy	GBR	Yamaha	0	0	0
29	17	de Reuver, Marc	NED	KTM	0	0	0
30	56	Priem, Manuel	BEL	Suzuki	0	0	0
31	5	Bartolini, Andrea	ITA	Yamaha	0	0	0
32	49	Goncalves, Rui	POR	Yamaha	0	0	0

MX2 World Championship standings:

Sword 197, Townley 194, Rattray 152, McFarlane 150, Maschio 124, de Reuver 121, Cairoli 114, Dobb 105, Leok 93, Nunn 91, Federici 78, Chiodi 71, Pourcel 62, Philippaerts 61, Barragan 58, Leuret 51, Dement 50, Boissiere 49, van Daele 47, Priem 42, Bartolini 41, Caps 40, Mackenzie 33, Swanepoel 29, Church 26, Goncalves 25, Cepelak 22, Monni 16, Nagl 13, Cherubini 9, Avis 8, Stevanini 7, Letellier 6, Salaets 5, Allier 4, Smith 4, Barreda 3, Seronval 3, Bernardez 2, Kulhavy 2, Campano 1, Vromans 1.

round six
Grand Prix of Benelux
Lichtenvoorde, 15-16 May 2004

After the circuit had emptied in Germany, a two-week hiatus preceded a leap back into the sand for the riders. The World Championships hadn't visited Lichtenvoorde (pronounced Lik-ten-vorda), tucked away in the eastern province of Gelderland, since 1996, but was now travelling to Holland for the second time in just over three weeks.

Perhaps the absence of de Reuver was a telling factor, but the crowds stayed away from the Benelux Grand Prix, with even the modest figure announced on Sunday of 10,000 for the weekend sounding exaggerated. It was a real pity because the track was interesting and well prepared, with its strange switch from sand to more gritty terrain in the woods acting as a novelty. The jumps were appealing enough on the flat bowl-like infield, and a large portion of the layout was easily visible; a distinct advantage over Valkenswaard. Sadly there wasn't any atmosphere. In six rounds this was the third stop in the Benelux and it already felt like overkill, with two more GPs in the region still left to run on the calendar. The Belgian riders were expressing their disappointment that the sand wasn't that deep, but it still looked an awful lot rougher and trickier than Valkenswaard. The technicians in 'Tyre alley' (the lengthy row of Michelin, Dunlop, Pirelli and Bridgestone rigs) were busy with heated cutters, slicing the knobs from the wheels into half their original size with an added scoop effect so as to churn the sand and increase traction.

The playing field was again slightly more level between 2-strokes and 4-strokes, and the rider who gained the most from some of the liberties afforded by the sand was Tanel Leok. The unassuming but hard-as-nails Estonian had been steering a Suzuki RM 250 machine for the British Motovision team since the start of the year. The bike had taken two World Championships in three years before 2003 in the hands of Pichon and was proving to be an apt foil for the nineteen-year-old. Leok was verifying his talent against the odds in the premier class and seemed to have found his niche in the small homely confines of the Motovision set-up. At Lichtenvoorde he would qualify sixth and take results of tenth and sixth for seventh overall; humbling a multitude of the 4-stroke army and continuing to do so in various subsequent GPs.

The casualty list increased early on Saturday. De Reuver had discovered his back-break and was in hospital recovering from surgery. Gundersen was unable to compete due to his knee injury. The high-profile KTM duo were joined by none other than the conqueror of Teutschenthal, Brian Jorgensen, who crashed in free practice and dislocated his shoulder. Pichon was now carrying the weight of the Italian Tiscali Martin team on his own damaged upper body.

Lichtenvoorde would stand as the venue at which Kevin Strijbos finally obtained his debut podium and ignited a path of recognition that will surely lead to many more trophies in the copious years he has ahead. Javier Garcia Vico and Thomas Traversini were still running blank Hondas, but further tests had taken place with the curious Aprilia, and an eagerly awaited premiere lay in store at the Italian Grand Prix in a month's time. The Maddi team would refrain from entering the two following rounds in order to prepare for the race at the Gallarate circuit. The Benelux Grand Prix was another successful exercise for Townley and Everts. Their respective 'doubles' officially slid both protagonists forward as championship favourites.

Saturday

Sunshine greeted the wide, open expanses of the grassy paddock at Lichtenvoorde but it was not to be a happy morning for Jorgensen. The number '8' machine threw its rider into the sand after only three laps during the first free practice session and the subsequent dislocation meant he would have to miss another race with a view to returning half-fit to the following Grand Prix (well, it worked the last time). 'I cannot believe my luck; one week a double winner and now looking at another injury,' he said. 'This track is so slippery. Normally at most places you can let the bike run through the rut but I hit a bump and the front wheel dug-in before I could react and it threw me over the bars. The doctors told me that I shouldn't ride while another opinion said it was possible, but there was a chance that the shoulder could pop out again. If I was racing then I would be only able to fight for something like fifteenth.'

Ken de Dijcker, Steve Ramon and Joel Smets were happy to decree the leading MX1 practice times throughout the morning and early afternoon. The chrono was exciting with Smets and a weakened Pichon recording their fastest laps as the clock clicked down to 'zero'. The Suzuki man was able to seal his first pole by less than half a second from the Frenchman. Pichon had no trouble handling the bike for several circulations but, not having trained for the last week and being unsure of competing ten days prior due to the after-effects of the German smash, was dubious as to his ability to gain a quality finish on Sunday. Everts' and Ramon's placings meant there were four different manufacturers in the top five.

The first MX2 heat saw a nasty tangle coming off the main jump on the infield and recent 'podiumees' Chiodi and Federici came off the worst. Federici's leg was struck by one of the cartwheeling machines and the ensuing pain would cancel out his fight for consecutive top-three results. Jonathan Barragan and Cairoli offered a surprising but decent scrap for second place (behind Townley naturally), eventually earned by the Spaniard. Townley had some complaints about the speed of the KTM in the sand but it was hard to sympathise, such was his authority on the terrain. His determination to rebuff the hard injustice of the German second-moto 'slap in the face' was clear to see. Luckily for Ben, the arrival of a sandy track was ideal timing for a reassertion of his championship credentials. Quiet Belgian Patrick Caps was beginning to surface after a poor start to the season and a lengthy period of adjustment on the Yamaha 250 4-stroke for the Evolution team. The manner of his dismissal of Andrew McFarlane's holeshot and early lead in the second MX2 moto was impressive and more reminiscent of the rider who challenged for the 2002 125cc World Championship. Caps, shy to the point of monosyllabic, was at home in the deeper sand and placed himself back in the frame for podium honours. Sword and Rattray had fallen on the second corner but both were able to take positions in the top five and not overly inhibit their gate positions.

Sunday

The opening MX1 moto was a belter. Five riders jostled for the lead, tripping each other up for numerous laps. The squabble for first position extended right until the final circulation when Everts used his experience to hold off the unusually combative Ramon by under two seconds. The KTM rider lost the lead and, in truth, the race with a mistake through the whoops less than ten minutes before the end. After the moto Strijbos was seething. Both Suzukis led the field early on after Strijbos had holeshotted, and while Smets slipped off twice in an

error-strewn run to fifth position, Strijbos never left the top three until four laps from the flag. Everts and Ramon had stretched away but the teenager was baulked by a backmarker in the closing moments, which allowed Melotte to catch him and pull off a daring overtaking move for third.

Bad luck turned into good fortune in a less-thrilling second outing as Strijbos benefited from Ramon's mechanical trouble to ease to his first ever World Championship podium. Everts was not keen on company for this race and the excitement was left to a stewed scrap between the Suzuki youngster and Melotte, with the Yamaha man again finishing just ahead. The L&M boys added more silverware for Team Rinaldi in what was a great result for Melotte, especially considering the speedy crash he suffered during practice on Saturday. Leok dazzled with his sixth position on the 250 in front of Vico, whose seventh place would be the last points scored by the jolly Spaniard in 2004. Pichon was not able to affect the skirmishes for the podium happening just in front of him, but fourth position overall was fine point-grabbing work in the circumstances. In a state of further come-down for Honda after Germany, Coppins also had another largely anonymous meeting. The twenty-eight-year-old mistimed the gate drop twice and 'rode like crap' by his own admission in the first moto.

The MX2 races were all about Ben and Tyla. Cairoli was a force almost equal to his more experienced peers and pushed Rattray hard in the second moto when Townley had disappeared into the distance. The opening race was more exciting when Rattray recovered from an unremarkable start and tried with all his might to square with Townley. The South African drew level several times but didn't quite have the necessary 'oomph' to seize control of the race. Sword bothered the threesome in the first moto but a bout of flu for several days in the week blunted his podium record as he couldn't live with the leaders. Caps even had the temerity to pass the championship leader for fourth. Townley, still in the midst of negotiations and speculation regarding the team with whom his future laid, continued his one hundred per cent winning streak in Holland, although his ever-critical eye wasn't over-enthused with his performance: 'Today was hard for me because I did not have a good feeling all weekend. I managed to ride consistently for both motos and eventually found a rhythm. It was tough and demanding out there, especially at the end of the day but that's good; I like to race in those conditions.' The second double nevertheless placed the New Zealander back at the top of the championship.

motocross
2004 Grand Prix Review

MX1

Overall Position	No.	Rider	Nat.	Bike	Race 1 Pos (Pts)	Race 2 Pos (Pts)	Total
1	72	Everts, Stefan	BEL	Yamaha	1 (25)	1 (25)	50
2	7	Melotte, Cedric	BEL	Yamaha	3 (20)	2 (22)	42
3	24	Strijbos, Kevin	BEL	Suzuki	4 (18)	3 (20)	38
4	2	Pichon, Mickael	FRA	Honda	6 (15)	4 (18)	33
5	31	Coppins, Joshua	NZL	Honda	7 (14)	5 (16)	30
6	6	Garcia Vico, Francisco	SPA	Honda	8 (13)	7 (14)	27
7	40	Leok, Tanel	EST	Suzuki	10 (11)	6 (15)	26
8	48	Burnham, Christian	GBR	KTM	9 (12)	9 (12)	24
9	74	Freibergs, Lauris	LAT	Honda	11 (10)	8 (13)	23
10	11	Ramon, Steve	BEL	KTM	2 (22)	0	22
11	12	Theybers, Danny	BEL	Yamaha	13 (8)	11 (10)	18
12	77	Kovalainen, Marko	FIN	Honda	12 (9)	14 (7)	16
13	3	Smets, Joel	BEL	Suzuki	5 (16)	0	16
14	27	Atsuta, Yoshitaka	JPN	Honda	15 (6)	13 (8)	14
15	26	Pyrhonen, Antti	FIN	Suzuki	14 (7)	15 (6)	13
16	80	de Dijcker, Ken	BEL	Honda	0	10 (11)	11
17	214	Engwall, Tommy	SWE	Suzuki	16 (5)	16 (5)	10
18	34	Noble, James	GBR	Honda	0	12 (9)	9
19	123	Oddenino, Enrico	ITA	TM	0	17 (4)	4
20	101	Robins, Erwin	NED	Yamaha	20 (1)	18 (3)	4
21	43	Meo, Antoine	FRA	Kawasaki	17 (4)	0	4
22	221	van den Berg, Heikki	NED	Yamaha	19 (2)	20 (1)	3
23	36	Flockhart, Stuart	GBR	Honda	18 (3)	0	3
24	220	Das, Michael	NED	Honda	0	19 (2)	2
25	216	Nambotin, Christophe	FRA	Yamaha	0	0	0
26	73	Traversini, Thomas	ITA	Honda	0	0	0
27	97	Breugelmans, Sven	BEL	KTM	0	0	0
28	208	Boekhorst, Gert Jan	NED	KTM	0	0	0
29	50	Hucklebridge, Mark	GBR	KTM	0	0	0
30	18	Bervoets, Marnicq	BEL	Yamaha	0	0	0

MX1 World Championship standings:

Everts 268, Melotte 230, Ramon 184, Pichon 183, Coppins 177, Smets 154, Strijbos 150, Gundersen 133, Leok 121, Garcia Vico 111, Jorgensen 110, de Dijcker 95, Atsuta 81, Freibergs 75, Theybers 74, Burnham 73, Bervoets 71, Pyrhonen 60, Noble 56, Kovalainen 47, Cooper 42, Martin 31, Hucklebridge 25, Seguy 21, Traversini 10, Engwall 10, Dugmore 9, Dobes 8, Meo 8, Breugelmans 7, Turpin 5, Flockhart 5, Robins 5, Oddenino 4, Dini 3, van den Berg 3, Das 2, Verhoeven 1.

MX2

Overall Position	No.	Rider	Nat.	Bike	Race 1 Pos (Pts)	Race 2 Pos (Pts)	Total
1	30	Townley, Ben	NZL	KTM	1 (25)	1 (25)	50
2	16	Rattray, Tyla	RSA	KTM	2 (22)	2 (22)	44
3	222	Cairoli, Antonio	ITA	Yamaha	3 (20)	3 (20)	40
4	37	Caps, Patrick	BEL	Yamaha	4 (18)	4 (18)	36
5	19	Sword, Stephen	GBR	Kawasaki	5 (16)	6 (15)	31
6	4	Chiodi, Alessio	ITA	Yamaha	8 (13)	5 (16)	29
7	15	McFarlane, Andrew	AUS	Yamaha	6 (15)	7 (14)	29
8	55	Nunn, Carl	GBR	Honda	10 (11)	10 (11)	22
9	83	Barragan, Jonathan	SPA	KTM	13 (8)	9 (12)	20
10	76	Leok, Aigar	EST	KTM	11 (10)	13 (8)	18
11	87	Dement, Jeff	USA	Honda	12 (9)	15 (6)	15
12	64	Dobb, James	GBR	Honda	9 (12)	18 (3)	15
13	121	Salaets, Kristof	BEL	Honda	7 (14)	0	14
14	68	Philippaerts, David	ITA	KTM	0	8 (13)	13
15	114	Swanepoel, Garreth	RSA	KTM	0	11 (10)	10
16	66	Stevanini, Christian	ITA	Honda	15 (6)	17 (4)	10
17	38	van Daele, Marvin	BEL	Suzuki	0	12 (9)	9
18	56	Priem, Manuel	BEL	Suzuki	19 (2)	14 (7)	9
19	49	Goncalves, Rui	POR	Yamaha	17 (4)	16 (5)	9
20	229	van Vijfeijken, Rob	NED	Yamaha	14 (7)	20 (1)	8
21	70	Church, Tom	GBR	Kawasaki	16 (5)	0	5
22	46	Guarnieri, Davide	ITA	KTM	18 (3)	0	3
23	65	Monni, Manuel	ITA	Yamaha	0	19 (2)	2
24	22	Federici, Claudio	ITA	Yamaha	20 (1)	0	1
25	71	Maschio, Mickael	FRA	Kawasaki	0	0	0
26	227	Strik, George	NED	KTM	0	0	0
27	99	Vromans, Oscar	NED	Yamaha	0	0	0
28	90	Pourcel, Sebastien	FRA	Kawasaki	0	0	0
29	92	Cherubini, Luca	ITA	Suzuki	0	0	0
30	226	de Belder, Tom	BEL	Honda	0	0	0

MX2 World Championship standings:

Townley 244, Sword 228, Rattray 196, McFarlane 179, Cairoli 154, Maschio 124, de Reuver 121, Dobb 120, Nunn 113, Leok 111, Chiodi 100, Federici 79, Barragan 78, Caps 76, Philippaerts 74, Dement 65, Pourcel 62, van Daele 56, Leuret 51, Priem 51, Boissiere 49, Bartolini 41, Swanepoel 39, Goncalves 34, Mackenzie 33, Church 31, Cepelak 22, Salaets 19, Monni 18, Stevanini 17, Nagl 13, Cherubini 9, van Vijfeijken 8, Avis 8, Letellier 6, Allier 4, Smith 4, Guarnieri 3, Barreda 3, Seronval 3, Bernardez 2, Kulhavy 2, Campano 1, Vromans 1.

British Grand Prix

Arreton, Isle of Wight, 29-30 May 2004

Stefan Everts was not a candidate for victory in Britain but enjoyed playing to the many fans.

British Grand Prix
Arreton, Isle of Wight, 29-30 May 2004

Numerous factors conspired to make the British Grand Prix the best round of the 2004 World Championship. A combination of good fortune and careful preparation assisted enormously to create a first-class motocross spectacle. The British public had been starved of GP action for four years, mainly due to the lack of a decent location (Foxhill had passed its sell-by date) and a club with enough financial clout to capture the rights and stage an event. Motivated by the knowledge that their Gore-Basin circuit on the Isle of Wight had been highly rated by all that had raced and seen the layout since its renovation and inauguration the previous year, multi-millionaire property developer Rob Bradley and his RTT racing team set about restoring one of the most historical and traditional Grand Prix. Track designer Johnny Douglas Hamilton demonstrated a shrewd eye, keenly influenced by the top-class American venues, in creating a special course that was quick, technically fulfilling and varied. 'The track here is just awesome; there are a lot of jumps and technical sections and it is fun,' said Strijbos. 'The track is very nice, like an American circuit with lots of jumps and air time,' remarked Andrew McFarlane. 'It is fast and physically demanding, the mud gets very rough with the braking bumps.' 'I love this track; it is very technical and suits me. It really makes you think and gives you a lot of air time,' said Tyla Rattray. 'The triple step-up just after the start is special for me,' said Sword. 'To holeshot around the first turn and come into there hearing the crowd behind you was the best feeling. It is a spectacular feature and there was a point in the second moto where Ben Townley and I jumped together after the start and looked right at each other.' 'The "rollers" at the top are the best part of the track. There are not many places like that in the World Championship,' offered Ben Townley.

The mud was choppy but grippy thanks to the constant watering, and lines started to spring up. With an exceptional rhythm section at the highest point and some well-placed jumps, Hamilton and his small crew had the majority of the paddock singing their praises by the end of Saturday's practice and qualifying.

Situated in the pleasant Arreton Downs, fifteen minutes from the ferry port in Cowes, the circuit used one side of a sloping gully to allow maximum viewing opportunities and was splendidly scenic to boot.

Pichon and Coppins go head-to-head in a thrilling second moto. Coppins is about to reach for a tear-off visor.

The likelihood of a rousing home victory was also an important aspect. Sword was easily the most popular rider over the weekend. His eventual third position would be his fifth trophy of the season and best ever result at his native round. He would push Townley and Rattray doggedly during the motos but an engine stall and the speed of the KTMs would prevent a dizzying triumph. The Grand Prix also produced the highest attendance of the year. The narrow country-lane access roads were packed getting into the circuit, and more people turned up to watch on Saturday than over the entire weekend at Lichtenvoorde. The eventual number clocked through the gate was 33,000, with a hefty amount filling the adjacent campsites. The event fell on a bank holiday weekend and was also blessed with some fantastic weather as sunshine and high temperatures gracing the two days of action. Expectation, an excellent circuit, good chances of home success, packed ferries bringing the hordes of fans, hot sunshine and a sense of occasion; the British Grand Prix was simply a winner. The final crowning element was some exciting racing which came as a natural by-product of the track.

It wasn't all perfect though. The sanitary provisions were nowhere near enough to accommodate the amount of visitors and the trip to the Island presented its own economic and logistical difficulties. Local ferry firms proved to be an invaluable ally with discounts and special trips transporting the paddock infrastructure (diligently brought and assembled at each GP by Belgian firm Maris)

from mainland England. The GP was not the cheapest motor sport event in the UK because of the travelling, but the crowd numbers gave a healthy pH test as to the large following that Motocross has in Britain but is rarely seen or read about.

Cedric Melotte journeyed over the water in some discomfort after a fast crash while training during the week. The Belgian had to be taken to a hospital in Parma, Italy after injuring his back. An X-ray confirmed no broken bones but the twenty-six-year-old would be lucky to gain another podium on the demanding Gore-Basin terrain. Gordon Crockard was making his first visit to a Grand Prix since the aborted attempt at Zolder and although walking normally after the ligament operation, was still several months away from a return to two wheels. Crockard held a press conference on Saturday evening to stress that he wasn't going to be rushed back to racing, but at the same time whispers were first starting to circulate that the likeable and witty Irishman was out of the CAS team he helped establish with his results in 2000 and 2001. Crockard had personal backing from energy drink company Red Bull, and the team had just signed an agreement with rival firm Sobe, throwing the two parties into a clash. Whether this mooted reason would eventually be the cause for the split is open to debate; it could be that Honda had simply lost patience with him after two empty seasons wrecked by injury. Nevertheless Crockard was among the first of the top riders to start assessing his options for 2005.

As one rider was outlining his plans for a comeback from a serious knee problem, another member of the MX1 series was preparing to leave and enter his own necessary phase of rehab. Joel Smets had reached round seven of the championship with reasonable success but his achievements paled in comparison to his own expectations. In pain on Sunday night and after finally deciding that he could not improve his condition any further, the thirty-four-year-old opted for an operation and hobbled away from 2004. Only one week later Smets would have to deal with a far more serious predicament regarding his health.

Jamie Dobb widened speculation of a rumoured retirement at the season's end by stating his desire for a good result at what could be 'his last British Grand Prix'. Dobb had been in his best shape for almost two seasons at the start of the year but results on the 250cc Honda in a return to the class he dominated in 2001 had not been forthcoming. There was some doubt as to whether Dobb still had the motivation after a long and eventful career in the sport. The bike had proven to be reliable but had yet to be seen at the front of a Grand Prix moto. Was it capable? The doubts were disproved at Gore-Basin, to the disillusionment of regular campaigners Nunn, Jeff Dement and Dobb but to the relief of Honda

Left: Josh Coppins finally gets to walk the top step.
Left below: Sword and Carl Nunn battle for positions in front of an expectant home crowd.

bosses in front of a British market where the marque is especially strong in sales. The bike led briefly in the first moto thanks to the efforts of wild-card entry Akira Narita. The Japanese AMA regular was guest of the CAS squad and riding the dusty CRF 250F vacated by Jussi Vehvilanen back in February, after the luckless Finn had crashed for the second consecutive year during pre-season and broken his back. Narita showed the aggression that serves as a pre-requisite in the ultra-tough American series but didn't quite have the durability to last the motos.

The British Grand Prix belonged very much to the people who made it; both in creation and the attendance. But the headlines were grabbed by yet another debut winner in the form of Josh Coppins, who leapt back to form in impeccable style, ending a ten-year wait for the 'top-step experience'. With Townley also faultless, it was a day of celebration for Kiwi motocross.

Saturday

Stefan Everts was taking his time finding speed on the track and his lowest positions of the season in practice (eighth, in both sessions) would be the first signs that the champion was not having his best weekend; although he dialled himself in for qualifying and was able to take second, seven-tenths from the pole time. Tanel Leok was again making a name for himself. The 250cc rider recorded the fastest lap at his team's home Grand Prix during the morning session and then was third in the second outing. After the flurry of attempts late in the chrono, the Estonian seemed very content with sixth entry in the gate for Sunday, wedged between the two factory Suzuki 450s of Strijbos and Smets. Brian Jorgensen had returned to the fold but his chances of another striking comeback akin to Teutschenthal seemed remote with practice and qualifying times almost two seconds off the pace. Pichon still did not have a perfect condition for Grand Prix motos but hard evidence of his path to recovery was witnessed in Timed Practice when he seemed more like his usual rapid self. A fifth pole position of the season duly fell in his direction. Josh Coppins was third, in front of Ramon, and the last rider in the 2 min. 5 secs bracket. Townley was immediately at home on the Gore-Basin bumps and had little difficulty, taking pole and his sixth qualification-heat win. Rattray was also enjoying the circuit and his quickest lap was within the same second as Townley.

Britain's last World Champion Jamie Dobb takes a farewell bow at his final home Grand Prix.

motocross
2004 Grand Prix Review

The pair separated themselves early on from the chasing Carl Nunn and Mickael Maschio. Sword created a buzz around the circuit in the next one by rapidly gobbling ground on the lengthy uphill start-straight and hitting the first right turn with the holeshot. He then pulled away to victory and second spot on the line for Sunday ahead of Narita and Pourcel in what was the easier qualifying race of the two. The hopes of the watching public had climbed even further.

The shock of the day in the MX2 class was the qualifying misery of Antonio Cairoli. The Italian swallowed some plastic fencing with his rear wheel in the second heat that necessitated a retirement after one lap. On a rough and difficult track for the Last Chance session, Cairoli faced stern opposition from Bartolini and Caps among others, and his best lap was seven-tenths of a second away from the top six. The teenager would have to join the bounteous British throng if he was to enjoy Sunday's races.

Sunday

It was a historic day for Josh Coppins and probably the most memorable moto finale of the season. When the closely pursuing and on-the-limit Mickael Pichon made an error through desperation on the last lap trying to draw alongside leader Coppins, it gave the Kiwi the precious breather he needed in the latter half of the second moto to win the race, and his first overall Grand Prix trophy. Up until the crescendo that divulged Pichon's wobble on the 'rollers', the moto had been building into a tense affair. It was definitely a good day for Honda. The Frenchman had taken the first moto from Coppins after the pair had divorced themselves from Ramon in third and a wanting Everts. The second race was again a Pichon-Coppins chase but this time the number 2 machine was not being handled as ruthlessly. Coppins made a superb move to seize the lead on the inside of the uphill triple and Pichon paused from the intensity of the dice in which he was making more mistakes. By the last-third distance he had found his composure and started to take chunks out of Coppins' advantage. Late into the race, and sensing this was the nearest he had ever come to his GP destiny, Coppins' determination on the bike was readily identifiable. The crowd sensed a tight finish and rallied for the Kiwi underdog. With two laps to go the Hondas were wheel-to-wheel, with Pichon looking for the slightest gap. One pass would mean victory. Coppins concentrated on his lines and left the panic up to his 'shadow'. Pichon couldn't squeeze past and his frantic effort to find more speed launching through the jump section at the top of the track was the defining moment, a mere five corners from the chequered flag.

The Honda's capabilities at the front of a race were briefly shown by Akira Narita.

Everts benefited from Ramon clipping a hay bale and crashing to take third and another podium. It was a bad day for Suzuki. Both Strijbos and Smets fell in the first moto, with only Smets able to make the finish. Better results arrived later in the afternoon but it was a GP to forget for the Belgian crew. The sterling efforts of Leok rescued some saving grace for the yellow brand with a double brace of fifth positions delivering his personal-best GP placing of fourth overall. Melotte was understandably lacklustre and just tried to survive. The first moto was his only high point with another fall, this time right next to the pits, giving him sixteenth in the second. Gundersen had returned but a crash in the first race caused further pain to his leg and he sat out the second.

Gore-Basin presented the fifth different winner in seven MX1 races and although Everts had been the only competitor showing title-winning composure so far, the class was producing some open and delectable moments. The Yamaha rider's advantage had now expanded to fifty-six points over Melotte. 'I don't really know what to say,' Coppins struggled after the podium ceremony. 'It has taken so long and has been too long. I have been close before and I have had more "seconds" than I can remember; I'm so happy to have finally won.'

For once the MX2 motos were overshadowed by MX1 for racing thrills. Sword tried his best to please the many willing fans but could not stop Townley's current juggernaut of form. The first moto of the day took place in front of a packed circuit primed and poised. The sound of the 250s' thump and 125s' whine was drowned by noise and air horns as Sword holeshotted and led up the hill into the tricky step-up triple. His status as leader of the British GP was to be short-lived after a mistake landing off a long jump saw the Kawasaki cut-out and Townley, along with four other riders, swept past before he could restart with one kick. Sword recovered to pass Narita and McFarlane for third but the KTMs had left the building in a repeat of their Lichtenvoorde showing in which Rattray would get as close as possible to Townley but would not be able to supersede him. The second moto was almost a repeat but the track was substantially rougher and forced more mistakes. Sword again led through the first turn and a nice moment was shared on the uphill triple as, level with Townley, both glanced across at the other in a brief gesture of friendly defiance. Townley stated after Moto1 that he expected Sword to come out with all guns blazing for the next race, and the Kawasaki rider duly gave all he had, but was not able to contain the orange duo. A dream victory turned into a satisfactory podium as the moto dragged towards its conclusion. Carl Nunn was second-highest Brit at RTT's home event. The fifth GP win for Townley arrived thanks to his tenth moto success and gave him a twenty-six-point margin over Sword in the standings. Perennial top-five lurker McFarlane was powerless to resist a Sword comeback in the first moto and suffered from not making a decisive move on Narita. The Australian rode his way through some incorrect suspension settings in the second race but was still disappointed with ninth. Billy Mackenzie made a comeback to GP action after his acrobatic crash at Teutschenthal and a first moto finish of tenth was a pleasing result.

Rob Bradley had mentioned before the Grand Prix that he felt Gore-Basin could be one of the best tracks in the World Championship. With the thousands of fans,

Sword gave his fans a podium result on Sunday but it could have been more if the Kawasaki had not stalled.

compliments and vast amounts of back slaps after the bank holiday weekend, his vision was nearer truth than he could have imagined. The British Grand Prix had returned and in style; the bar had been lifted for other clubs and circuits to take note. Perhaps it is not too ridiculous to declare that the work and effort placed into the circuit was like a major shot in the arm for World Championship motocross. If the other fifteen venues could adopt a similar 'track-first' philosophy, as shown at Gore-Basin, then the level of skill, reputation and general regard of the Grand Prix series would easily go on to reach new heights.

motocross
2004 Grand Prix Review

MX1

Overall Position	No.	Rider	Nat.	Bike	Race 1 Pos (Pts)	Race 2 Pos (Pts)	Total
1	31	**Coppins, Joshua**	NZL	Honda	2 (22)	1 (25)	47
2	2	**Pichon, Mickael**	FRA	Honda	1 (25)	2 (22)	47
3	72	**Everts, Stefan**	BEL	Yamaha	4 (18)	3 (20)	38
4	40	**Leok, Tanel**	EST	Suzuki	5 (16)	5 (16)	32
5	11	**Ramon, Steve**	BEL	KTM	3 (20)	12 (9)	29
6	80	**de Dijcker, Ken**	BEL	Honda	8 (13)	7 (14)	27
7	18	**Bervoets, Marnicq**	BEL	Yamaha	7 (14)	9 (12)	26
8	28	**Seguy, Luigi**	FRA	Yamaha	10 (11)	10 (11)	22
9	3	**Smets, Joel**	BEL	Suzuki	15 (6)	6 (15)	21
10	34	**Noble, James**	GBR	Honda	11 (10)	11 (10)	20
11	7	Melotte, Cedric	BEL	Yamaha	6 (15)	16 (5)	20
12	24	Strijbos, Kevin	BEL	Suzuki	0	4 (18)	18
13	8	Jorgensen, Brian	DEN	Honda	0	8 (13)	13
14	36	Flockhart, Stuart	GBR	Honda	16 (5)	13 (8)	13
15	77	Kovalainen, Marko	FIN	Honda	9 (12)	0	12
16	123	Oddenino, Enrico	ITA	TM	17 (4)	14 (7)	11
17	48	Burnham, Christian	GBR	KTM	13 (8)	19 (2)	10
18	27	Atsuta, Yoshitaka	JPN	Honda	12 (9)	0	9
19	247	Rose, Jordan	GBR	Yamaha	19 (2)	15 (6)	8
20	43	Meo, Antoine	FRA	Kawasaki	14 (7)	0	7
21	216	Nambotin, Christophe	FRA	Yamaha	20 (1)	17 (4)	5
22	246	Campbell, David	GBR	Honda	18 (3)	20 (1)	4
23	326	Poikela, Hannu	FIN	Suzuki	0	18 (3)	3
24	10	Gundersen, Kenneth	NOR	KTM	0	0	0
25	120	Dugmore, Collin	RSA	Honda	0	0	0
26	74	Freibergs, Lauris	LAT	Honda	0	0	0
27	50	Hucklebridge, Mark	GBR	KTM	0	0	0

MX1 World Championship standings:

Everts 306, Melotte 250, Pichon 230, Coppins 224, Ramon 213, Smets 175, Strijbos 168, Leok 153, Gundersen 133, Jorgensen 123, de Dijcker 122, Garcia Vico 111, Bervoets 97, Atsuta 90, Burnham 83, Noble 76, Freibergs 75, Theybers 74, Pyrhonen 60, Kovalainen 59, Seguy 43, Cooper 42, Martin 31, Hucklebridge 25, Flockhart 18, Meo 15, Oddenino 15, Traversini 10, Engwall 10, Dugmore 9, Rose 8, Dobes 8, Breugelmans 7, Nambotin 5, Turpin 5, Robins 5, Campbell 4, Poikela 3, Dini 3, van den Berg 3, Das 2, Verhoeven 1.

MX2

Overall Position	No.	Rider	Nat.	Bike	Race 1 Pos (Pts)	Race 2 Pos (Pts)	Total
1	30	**Townley, Ben**	NZL	KTM	1 (25)	1 (25)	50
2	16	**Rattray, Tyla**	RSA	KTM	2 (22)	2 (22)	44
3	19	**Sword, Stephen**	GBR	Kawasaki	3 (20)	3 (20)	40
4	71	**Maschio, Mickael**	FRA	Kawasaki	5 (16)	6 (15)	31
5	369	**Narita, Akira**	JPN	Honda	9 (12)	4 (18)	30
6	15	**McFarlane, Andrew**	AUS	Yamaha	4 (18)	9 (12)	30
7	55	**Nunn, Carl**	GBR	Honda	6 (15)	7 (14)	29
8	118	**Boissiere, Anthony**	FRA	Yamaha	8 (13)	11 (10)	23
9	64	**Dobb, James**	GBR	Honda	7 (14)	13 (8)	22
10	4	**Chiodi, Alessio**	ITA	Yamaha	11 (10)	10 (11)	21
11	37	Caps, Patrick	BEL	Yamaha	14 (7)	8 (13)	20
12	76	Leok, Aigar	EST	KTM	0	5 (16)	16
13	22	Federici, Claudio	ITA	Yamaha	19 (2)	12 (9)	11
14	211	Mackenzie, Billy	GBR	Yamaha	10 (11)	0	11
15	68	Philippaerts, David	ITA	KTM	13 (8)	20 (1)	9
16	90	Pourcel, Sebastien	FRA	Kawasaki	12 (9)	0	9
17	52	Leuret, Pascal	FRA	KTM	0	14 (7)	7
18	38	van Daele, Marvin	BEL	Suzuki	0	15 (6)	6
19	49	Goncalves, Rui	POR	Yamaha	20 (1)	16 (5)	6
20	242	Anderson, Brad	GBR	KTM	15 (6)	0	6
21	5	Bartolini, Andrea	ITA	Yamaha	18 (3)	19 (2)	5
22	56	Priem, Manuel	BEL	Suzuki	16 (5)	0	5
23	66	Stevanini, Christian	ITA	Honda	0	17 (4)	4
24	70	Church, Tom	GBR	Kawasaki	17 (4)	0	4
25	114	Swanepoel, Garreth	RSA	KTM	0	18 (3)	3
26	95	Nagl, Maximilian	GER	KTM	0	0	0
27	65	Monni, Manuel	ITA	Yamaha	0	0	0
28	711	Allier, Tomas	FRA	Kawasaki	0	0	0
29	83	Barragan, Jonathan	SPA	KTM	0	0	0
30	41	Letellier, Antoine	FRA	Suzuki	0	0	0
31	69	Avis, Wyatt	RSA	Suzuki	0	0	0

MX2 World Championship standings:

Townley 294, Sword 268, Rattray 240, McFarlane 209, Maschio 155, Cairoli 154, Dobb 142, Nunn 142, Leok 127, de Reuver 121, Chiodi 121, Caps 96, Federici 90, Philippaerts 83, Barragan 78, Boissiere 72, Pourcel 71, Dement 65, van Daele 62, Leuret 5, Priem 56, Bartolini 46, Mackenzie 44, Swanepoel 42, Goncalves 40, Church 35, Narita 30, Cepelak 22, Stevanini 21, Salaets 19, Monni 18, Nagl 13, Cherubini 9, van Vijfeijken 8, Avis 8, Anderson 6, Letellier 6, Allier 4, Smith 4, Guarnieri 3, Barreda 3, Seronval 3, Bernardez 2, Kulhavy 2, Campano 1, Vromans 1.

Grand Prix of France
St Jean D'Angely, 5-6 June 2004

Tyla Rattray was well placed once more to secure another win but this time a decent race in the second moto made the achievement sweeter.

round eight
round eight
Grand Prix of France
St Jean D'Angely, 29-30 May 2004

Another consecutive weekend of Grand Prix racing drew the riders to St Jean D'Angely in France for round eight. The meeting required a journey halfway down the country and towards the western coastal town of La Rochelle. The circuit is not too dissimilar in its sprawling geographic to Gore-Basin, with the track weaving its way across an incline on one side of a valley and the crowd grouped together on the opposing slant. However, unlike the Isle of Wight, St Jean D'Angely was a good example of a decent meeting being let down by the track. After years of use the venue had simply run out of mud. There was little to work with in terms of terrain, with the rocky ground poking through on the racing lines. The dirt slowly pushed its way to the sides of the track and a stony and slippery surface was all that remained. The course didn't have many jumps and a 100m-long sandpit at the top of the hill was a vast departure from the rest of the circuit; the zone would entertain the majority of the crashes over the weekend. With hot sunshine hardly helping matters it became a headache to try and contain the large plumes of dust that were billowing out on Saturday. Applying more water to the track was the only solution, but watering stone hardly created a safe or conducive environment for Grand Prix motocross. As ever, the helpful and friendly club at St Jean had put a lot of effort into the event. The Grand Prix was well-attended, as per usual in France, and the weather was again good. The temperatures reached the low 30s for the hottest day so far in the season. The aroma from the large barbecue stalls covered the west side of the circuit had the sweating journalists in the press room just above practically eating their mice.

Despite his electrifying part in the British GP extravaganza and subsequent podium result, Mickael Pichon was still far from content with his preparation. The injury to his shoulders in Germany was causing pain and limited his chances to train on the bike during the week. Thus his riding during the Grand Prix weekends had developed a slightly unpredictable edge, due to his lack of track time. Pichon's seventy-six-point deficit to Everts in the championship (effectively three motos) was a large distance to peg back at the halfway stage of the season. The twenty-eight-year-old, who had become remarkably more laid back and approachable this year, had admitted that he was now chasing podiums in an effort to regain whatever ground possible. Pichon is a closed guy who loves the company of his family. Usually one of the last to arrive in the living area on a Friday night, Mickael travels with his wife Stephanie (who was expecting their second child throughout the season), young son Zac, parents, sister and two dogs in tow. The fact that Pichon was showing signs of mellowing out could be seen as a result of the humbling knee injury towards the end of 2003, but the small character change was mainly attributed to the counsel and help of former World Champion Jacky Vimond. Acting as a coach and source of mental support to Pichon, Vimond was another of the friendly down-to-earth guys in the paddock and his quiet, calm approach to matters, not only racing related, was rubbing off on his confidante. One of Mickael's great qualities, and one that is rarely seen, is the amount of help and guidance he gives to younger riders. Strijbos owes his break in the Suzuki team thanks to the insistence of Pichon when the Frenchman was there in his title-winning pomp of 2001 and 2002. He also speaks regularly with French youngsters Nicolas Aubin, Pascal Leuret and Sebastien Pourcel, and can easily be spotted trackside during the MX2 sessions gesturing in encouragement. Pichon won the last Grand Prix at St Jean back in 2002 (250cc, as Everts won the 500cc contest on the same day) and while he would not be victorious on this occasion because of a rare mechanical failure, the Grand Prix of France would be the last time that Mickael would not mount a podium in 2004.

A former 250cc GP winner and now leading KTM's effort in the MX3 Championship, Yves Demaria was making an MX1 wild-card appearance at his home Grand Prix. Demaria showed some impressive speed, especially with third position behind Everts and Coppins in the second moto.

Some disturbing news filtered through late in the week regarding Joel Smets, who had been admitted to hospital not to undergo surgery on his knee, but for a stint in intensive care as the Belgian picked up a bacterial blood infection that had sent his temperature rocketing. For a fortnight Smets would be retained in a Belgian ward before finally being released. The course of antibiotics and recovery period would delay the knee operation and mean that Smets would not be sitting on a motorcycle until December. Another rider shortly to experience a series of hospital tests would be Billy Mackenzie, who had been out of sorts to the normal throttle-wringing rider the British fans have become accustomed to watching. Mackenzie finally reached a crucial point in his season at France after almost collapsing in the second moto. A gluten allergy diagnosis the following week

It doesn't quite go to plan for Sebastien Pourcel at his home GP.

(meaning the Scotsman had been stuffing his face with the wrong type of food) represented the first steps towards recovery and some good performances in the MX1 class later in the season.

Saturday

The long uphill drags and hard ground forced bike set-up and tyre selection to the fore more than any other Grand Prix of the seven so far. The 4-strokes would gain a better degree of traction and the hearts of the 125 and 250cc riders must have sunk a little upon arriving at the track Saturday morning under a bright blue sky.

Kenneth Gundersen was an absentee and the Norwegian's knee was taking longer to sort out than originally hoped. Josh Coppins was second fastest in both practice sessions and naturally on something of a high after conquering the Island. In official Timed Practice for the French GP MX1 gate, Mickael Pichon was able to bring his pole-position tally to six, after his fifth lap of seven attempts proved to be a second-and-a-half quicker than Steve Ramon's best. The KTM representative headed a group of six riders all within the same second, including the likes of Coppins, Strijbos and Leok down to Jorgensen. Leok was causing the scribes to exercise their knowledge of superlatives by maintaining his streak of form. Once again the Estonian had little right to be fighting for the positions

Pichon congratulates Everts after a hard first moto. Note the self-made jersey holes to help combat the heat.

he was reaching on the 250 but was handling the machine like an 80cc. His destination and employment for 2005 was starting to be a common theme of discussion among the paddock. One person assuring his short-term future was Ben Townley, who finally signed a new contract and unsurprisingly decided to stay with KTM, agreeing to give the MX1 class a shot in 2005 alongside Ramon

and Gundersen, before departing to the US and dreams of the AMA. In MX2 Sword and Townley renewed their rivalry from Gore-Basin for the first qualification heat. Sword again grabbed a holeshot but Townley captured the win in a familiar pattern. Federici, enjoying a hard surface not so different to his native Italian tracks, was third. Cairoli crashed out of eleventh place on the last lap but this

Despite the aerial show Brian Jorgensen was fighting to be fit at St Jean.

time made it through the Last Chance session in fourth spot. In the next race Sebastien Pourcel won his first ever qualification heat on the 250cc Kawasaki to enter the gate second and was encouraged by the distance of several seconds he managed to maintain over Rattray. Wild-card entry Christophe Pourcel had already been getting some rave reviews with his speed and ability in the 125cc

European Championship. The fifteen-year-old sibling of Sebastien (who modestly admitted that his younger brother was the real talent of the family) wasn't able to qualify via the heats, but was an impressive second position on the 2-stroke in the Last Chance to guarantee his first GP start.

A typical Pichon shape as he arcs over a jump but his second moto was swiftly ended by a stone.

Sunday

Tyla Rattray won his second career Grand Prix and also took the 'lowest moto position but overall winner' award for the season. After two rounds more or less following the form book the MX2 races were once more a mix of fortunes and jumble of results to decide the podium places. Rattray had a stinker of a start in the first moto and was as far down as fifteenth on the first lap. That he managed to come back to ninth spot and still take the overall 'top step' riding the 2-stroke spoke volumes of the spooky irregularity of the class. To be fair to 'Styla', who

was competing at one of his least favourite circuits, his second-race performance and subsequent victory was much better and his one-point overall advantage over Maschio, Chiodi and Federici, all hard-pack experts, left a satisfying taste after a debut moto win. So what happened to the others? Townley had won the first race after taking his time to pass holeshotter Cairoli, who enjoyed his longest stint at the front of a GP by leading for nine out of the eighteen laps. The Italian forgot his recent qualifying woe to chase the KTM all the way to the flag. Sword finished third in front of Federici and the Chiodi, the trio never coming into contact once. In the second race Townley surprisingly crashed while third and wading his way through the deep sand pit. The bike slid away from him and took an age to restart, by which time the Kiwi was long out of the reckoning. The track had been watered and the shiny rock yielded a slippery surface with the patches of mud now swamp-like. Sword was a first-lap crashee after his goggles had clogged with mud, and he slipped off just before the finish line. It was to be a difficult race for the Scot as he later stalled the bike and also twisted his weak ankle before giving up on the moto while out of the points positions. Rattray was able to pass Maschio at midway and win by four seconds. Maschio gave the home fans a podium from Chiodi who was making his second appearance of the year in the final top three. Townley was able to hang onto his championship lead after Sword's error but Rattray had gained ground in third. Anthony Boissiere took his highest moto position of the season with sixth in the second race, giving him the same standing overall. Dobb failed to finish both times after a first-corner crash also collected McFarlane, who was able to rescue one point for twentieth after pitting with a bent gear lever. The Aussie would have brake trouble in the second race and have to enter the pit lane on a more permanent basis.

Stefan Everts claimed a ninth French Grand Prix win of his career with a double moto haul, and benefited from some bad luck mechanically to both Mickael Pichon and Cedric Melotte to extend his Championship advantage. Coppins led the first race but his hopes of a swift British GP repeat were felled by Everts and then Pichon, as they both went by on lap six of nineteen. The Honda ace had simply pushed too hard too soon and needed to back off. Pichon was suffering with a tyre compound that was too hard and couldn't catch up to Everts. Melotte, feeling stronger after his painful UK experience, was fourth in front of Ramon and the determined home GP adrenaline charge of Luigi Seguy who had been contesting the season so far with a wrist injury.

Selecting a softer tyre for the second moto, Pichon signalled his intent from the gate drop. He and Everts started scrapping right from the first lap but the

Maschio on the edge. The 2002 World Champion emerged from early season obscurity to take second place overall on the Kawasaki.

intense action was short-lived as a stone smashed Pichon's front brake, causing the fluid to escape and giving the Frenchman no stopping power on the steep downhill drops. His frustration was evident and the team held a secret debrief after the heat in which a metal guard, to the expense of a single euro, would have prevented the damage. 'I was close to Stefan and could see that he was on the limit whereas I still had something left to give,' he reflected. 'I was feeling good and had a strong rhythm. I cannot say if I would have got him but I had a great chance and would have put him under a lot of pressure. I then got hit by a rock from Stefan's wheel and it smashed the front brake. The fluid drained out and I almost went into the fence on the downhill. There was not much I could do because I had no front brake at all.' Everts then had free reign with Coppins able

to relegate the spirited Demaria to third late into the moto. Ramon was fourth, collecting his second podium, and Tanel Leok completed a wonderful flight from thirteenth on the first lap to fifth. Japanese rider Yoshi Atsuta also recorded a season-high-to-date with sixth. Strijbos had his worst weekend of the year with a thirteenth in Moto2. The Belgian crashed and couldn't restart earlier in the day, while KTM MX3 rider Julien Bill knocked him off at the start of the second race. Those troublesome stones also ended Melotte's moto after ten laps when his titanium gear lever was bent by a flying rock.

The Grand Prix of France drew another sizeable crowd of nearly 29,000 people and World Championship motocross certainly had a lofty, feel-good factor finishing the first half of the year.

motocross
2004 Grand Prix Review

MX1

Overall Position	No.	Rider	Nat.	Bike	Race 1 Pos (Pts)	Race 2 Pos (Pts)	Total
1	72	Everts, Stefan	BEL	Yamaha	1 (25)	1 (25)	50
2	31	Coppins, Joshua	NZL	Honda	3 (20)	2 (22)	42
3	11	Ramon, Steve	BEL	KTM	5 (16)	4 (18)	34
4	28	Seguy, Luigi	FRA	Yamaha	6 (15)	7 (14)	29
5	40	Leok, Tanel	EST	Suzuki	11 (10)	5 (16)	26
6	8	Jorgensen, Brian	DEN	Honda	8 (13)	9 (12)	25
7	27	Atsuta, Yoshitaka	JPN	Honda	14 (7)	6 (15)	22
8	48	Burnham, Christian	GBR	KTM	10 (11)	10 (11)	22
9	2	Pichon, Mickael	FRA	Honda	2 (22)	0	22
10	78	Demaria, Yves	FRA	KTM	0	3 (20)	20
11	74	Freibergs, Lauris	LAT	Honda	15 (6)	8 (13)	19
12	33	Bethys, Thierry	FRA	Honda	13 (8)	11 (10)	18
13	7	Melotte, Cedric	BEL	Yamaha	4 (18)	0	18
14	77	Kovalainen, Marko	FIN	Honda	16 (5)	12 (9)	14
15	34	Noble, James	GBR	Honda	9 (12)	19 (2)	14
16	43	Meo, Antoine	FRA	Kawasaki	7 (14)	0	14
17	105	Bill, Julien	SUI	KTM	12 (9)	18 (3)	12
18	24	Strijbos, Kevin	BEL	Suzuki	0	13 (8)	8
19	216	Nambotin, Christophe	FRA	Yamaha	20 (1)	14 (7)	8
20	21	Dini, Fabrizio	ITA	KTM	18 (3)	16 (5)	8
21	123	Oddenino, Enrico	ITA	TM	0	15 (6)	6
22	255	Beaudouin, Raphael	FRA	Suzuki	0	17 (4)	4
23	80	de Dijcker, Ken	BEL	Honda	17 (4)	0	4
24	85	Turpin, Vincent	FRA	Honda	19 (2)	0	2
25	290	Lyons, Adam	IRL	Kawasaki	0	20 (1)	1
26	250	Lillywhite, Chris	GBR	VOR	0	0	0
27	207	Seronval, Steve	BEL	Yamaha	0	0	0
28	97	Breugelmans, Sven	BEL	KTM	0	0	0
29	18	Bervoets, Marnicq	BEL	Yamaha	0	0	0
30	258	Burkhart, Luke	NZL	Suzuki	0	0	0

MX2

Overall Position	No.	Rider	Nat.	Bike	Race 1 Pos (Pts)	Race 2 Pos (Pts)	To
1	16	Rattray, Tyla	RSA	KTM	9 (12)	1 (25)	3
2	71	Maschio, Mickael	FRA	Kawasaki	7 (14)	2 (22)	3
3	4	Chiodi, Alessio	ITA	Yamaha	5 (16)	3 (20)	3
4	22	Federici, Claudio	ITA	Yamaha	4 (18)	4 (18)	3
5	222	Cairoli, Antonio	ITA	Yamaha	2 (22)	10 (11)	3
6	118	Boissiere, Anthony	FRA	Yamaha	8 (13)	6 (15)	2
7	30	Townley, Ben	NZL	KTM	1 (25)	0	2
8	37	Caps, Patrick	BEL	Yamaha	10 (11)	9 (12)	2
9	76	Leok, Aigar	EST	KTM	13 (8)	8 (13)	2
10	19	Sword, Stephen	GBR	Kawasaki	3 (20)	0	2
11	55	Nunn, Carl	GBR	Honda	18 (3)	5 (16)	1
12	56	Priem, Manuel	BEL	Suzuki	16 (5)	7 (14)	1
13	68	Philippaerts, David	ITA	KTM	11 (10)	13 (8)	1
14	90	Pourcel, Sebastien	FRA	Kawasaki	6 (15)	19 (2)	1
15	95	Nagl, Maximilian	GER	KTM	15 (6)	11 (10)	1
16	83	Barragan, Jonathan	SPA	KTM	0	12 (9)	
17	52	Leuret, Pascal	FRA	KTM	12 (9)	0	
18	49	Goncalves, Rui	POR	Yamaha	19 (2)	15 (6)	
19	46	Guarnieri, Davide	ITA	KTM	0	14 (7)	
20	66	Stevanini, Christian	ITA	Honda	14 (7)	0	
21	251	Aubin, Nicolas	FRA	Kawasaki	0	16 (5)	
22	38	van Daele, Marvin	BEL	Suzuki	0	17 (4)	
23	65	Monni, Manuel	ITA	Yamaha	17 (4)	0	
24	377	Pourcel, Christophe	FRA	Kawasaki	0	18 (3)	
25	211	Mackenzie, Billy	GBR	Yamaha	0	20 (1)	
26	15	McFarlane, Andrew	AUS	Yamaha	20 (1)	0	
27	41	Letellier, Antoine	FRA	Suzuki	0	0	
28	5	Bartolini, Andrea	ITA	Yamaha	0	0	
29	711	Allier, Tomas	FRA	Kawasaki	0	0	
30	64	Dobb, James	GBR	Honda	0	0	

MX1 World Championship standings:

Everts 356, Melotte 268, Coppins 266, Pichon 252, Ramon 247, Leok 179, Strijbos 176, Smets 175, Jorgensen 148, Gundersen 133, de Dijcker 126, Atsuta 112, Garcia Vico 111, Burnham 105, Bervoets 97, Freibergs 94, Noble 90, Theybers 74, Kovalainen 73, Seguy 72, Pyrhonen 60, Cooper 42, Martin 31, Meo 29, Hucklebridge 25, Oddenino 21, Demaria 20, Bethys 18, Flockhart 18, Nambotin 13, Bill 12, Dini 11, Traversini 10, Engwall 10, Dugmore 9, Rose 8, Dobes 8, Breugelmans 7, Turpin 7, Robins 5, Beaudouin 4, Campbell 4, Poikela 3, van den Berg 3, Das 2, Verhoeven 1, Lyons 1.

MX2 World Championship standings:

Townley 319, Sword 288, Rattray 277, McFarlane 210, Maschio 191, Cairoli 187, Nunn 161, Chiodi 157, Leok 148, Dobb 142, Federici 126, de Reuver 121, Caps 119, Philippaerts 101, Boissiere 100, Pourcel 88, Barragan 8,7 Priem 75, Leuret 67, van Daele 66, Dement 65, Goncalves 48, Bartolini 46, Mackenzie 45, Swanepoel 42, Church 35, Narita 30, Nagl 29, Stevanini 28, Cepelak 22, Monni 22, Salaets 19, Guarnieri 10, Cherubini 9, van Vijfeijken 8, Avis 8, Anderson 6, Letellier 6, Aubin 5, Allier 4, Smith 4, Pourcel 3, Barreda 3, Seronval 3, Bernardez 2, Kulhavy 2, Campano 1, Vromans 1.

Grand Prix of Italy
Gallarate, Milan, 12-13 June 2004

Coppins adapted to the track instantly, setting lap times in the low 1 min. 50 secs. Pichon secured his seventh pole position with a circulation almost a second faster than Coppins. Everts was one-tenth slower than the CAS Honda rider with Leok now in customary 'wild-man mode' on the 250 and a phenomenal four-tenths of a second behind the eight-times World Champion. It was the Estonian's best qualification so far. Brian Jorgensen showed his experience of Italian tracks (the Dane had ridden for Italian teams for the last three seasons) to classify fifth in front of Strijbos on a warm day's work for all the riders. Aprilia sweated it out in nineteenth (Vico) and twenty-sixth.

Husqvarna held a press conference to announce their return to the World Championships in 2005 with the presentation also blending in news about Supermoto projects, which wasn't that interesting. The bilingual Aprilia conference was also a chore. After the novelty of gazing at the work of art that was the MXV, the one-hour event quickly took on snooze proportions. However it was interesting to see representatives from the Chinese Federation circling the paddock, increasing speculation that the World Championships would visit the country in the next two seasons.

Sunday

'I could not have asked for anything better of myself, the team and the race bike. I have been here in Europe for four years and it has been worth the wait to be one of the best riders to come from Australia and eventually take a double GP and overall win. I will treasure that. I know that the first eight GPs were not so special but I feel that I have reached a turning point and can build on this win today.' After bouncing around three teams in three years, Andrew McFarlane finally cast aside some of the doubts about his temperament and dedication at Gallarate when he glided to a double moto sweep. 'Sharky' was untouchable in the first MX2 race, leading from the opening corner over Patrick Caps for half the moto before Federici was able to rise to second. The track was pretty slippery on Sunday thanks to the organisers wary of the afternoon sun and wanting to prevent a dust cloud. Townley recovered from one of his worst starts of the year (it would get worse) to finish third in front of Sword, Caps and Chiodi while Cairoli struggled to come back from a first-lap position of thirteenth.

McFarlane's resurged confidence paid off in the second race when he took the lead in the final five laps after slowly building his speed from sixth. The race was an exciting mix of action and incident. Cairoli fired-up the crowd along with

Above: Camouflage. Pichon glances at a chasing Ramon in front of a packed and sunburnt Italian hillside.
Opposite above: Andrew McFarlane hovers around the circuit in a governing mood.
Opposite below: Strijbos beats former mentor Pichon for his second career podium.

Top: Antonio Cairoli discovers a new and sizeable fan club.
Bottom: Townley's least-effective weekend of the season occurred at Gallarate. Here he has gone down at the first turn with Federici.

countryman Chiodi and Mickael Maschio (who retired after a crash and then engine trouble in the first moto) in a battle for the lead until McFarlane clicked into gear. Chiodi and Federici would complete the podium to satisfy the noisy and appreciative watching multitude. Maschio fell again on the last lap trying to pass Chiodi for third and had to settle for fourth in front of Pourcel, who couldn't drag himself up into contention. Stephen Sword had originally holeshotted the race and held off Cairoli for the first five laps. The Kawasaki rider had a sign from the pits that Townley had gone down with Rattray in the first corner. The chance to settle into a groove and score a hatful of points never arrived as the 250 seized on the lip of a long steep drop and Sword had to bail over the bars to stop himself being flicked into the ground. The image was spectacular and violent. It was certainly one of the biggest crashes of the year and the collective gasp by the watching crowd of over 18,000 added extra gravitas. Luckily Sword was OK and actually checked his bike, that was a good fifty metres further along the track, to see if it could be restarted. It couldn't and, with Rattray having a nightmare of a weekend, Townley would turn an otherwise poor GP for him and the KTM into another point-collecting exercise. He could scarcely believe his fortune at the eleven-point increase to his advantage while the following three of Sword, Rattray and McFarlane had closed up, indicating a good run-in for the title.

Kevin Strijbos turned a holeshot and early lead into an MX1 moto victory; his '25-point' debut. The Suzuki rider finally made good on his threats to walk off with a race after coming close at Zolder and Bellpuig. The Belgian ploughed through the opening turn in first place for the umpteenth time this season thanks to a strong combination of technique and the Suzuki's power. What many thought would be the inevitable 'crumble' never arrived and the teenager was assisted greatly by Brian Jorgensen, who held up Pichon and Everts, even going so far as to get involved in some pushing and shoving with his teammate before being overtaken. It was a memorable race, not only for producing the seventh different moto winner of the year, but also for the intensity of the early fighting for second position. Diplomatically, Pichon hardly referred to the clashes with Jorgensen afterwards, but one could have easily imagined the colourful language echoing inside the Frenchman's lid at the time. With his shoulder still weak the Dane was little more than a mobile chicane and weathered the brief exchanges to take fifth. Another Ramon mistake three laps from the finish allowed Everts and Pichon to slip through but the Yamaha expert was not able to catch the Suzuki pilot, who had calmed down and accustomed himself to the fact that victory was

a possibility. Strijbos was grinning like a little boy at Christmas afterwards; fair enough, considering his tender years.

His start would be the polar opposite in the second moto when he got a little excited off the line and lost ground controlling a wheeling RM-Z. The next forty minutes were spent working his way up from eighteenth to finally depose Ramon of fourth and nudge Pichon to the third step of the podium. Everts stole a small march over Pichon and the duel for victory was a close one. The Belgian triumphed purely by his perfection; one error and Pichon would have taken the initiative. It was a vintage motocross performance on a track that was far from easy. The Honda rider could barely dent an infuriating cushion of just over two seconds. Coppins, who stalled the bike in the first moto after a poor tyre choice, made amends with third. Melotte was left haunting the top ten and Leok could not live up to his Saturday billing, finding the 4-strokes a tougher prospect than originally envisaged. Atsuta, Seguy and KTM rider Julien Bill also notched worthy results.

motocross
2004 Grand Prix Review

MX1

Overall Position	No.	Rider	Nat.	Bike	Race 1 Pos (Pts)	Race 2 Pos (Pts)	Total
1	72	Everts, Stefan	BEL	Yamaha	2 (22)	1 (25)	47
2	24	Strijbos, Kevin	BEL	Suzuki	1 (25)	4 (18)	43
3	2	Pichon, Mickael	FRA	Honda	3 (20)	2 (22)	42
4	31	Coppins, Joshua	NZL	Honda	6 (15)	3 (20)	35
5	11	Ramon, Steve	BEL	KTM	4 (18)	5 (16)	34
6	28	Seguy, Luigi	FRA	Yamaha	8 (13)	7 (14)	27
7	105	Bill, Julien	SUI	KTM	10 (11)	8 (13)	24
8	7	Melotte, Cedric	BEL	Yamaha	9 (12)	10 (11)	23
9	80	de Dijcker, Ken	BEL	Honda	11 (10)	9 (12)	22
10	40	Leok, Tanel	EST	Suzuki	7 (14)	14 (7)	21
11	8	Jorgensen, Brian	DEN	Honda	5 (16)	16 (5)	21
12	48	Burnham, Christian	GBR	KTM	12 (9)	12 (9)	18
13	27	Atsuta, Yoshitaka	JPN	Honda	20 (1)	6 (15)	16
14	75	Dobes, Josef	CZE	Suzuki	16 (5)	11 (10)	15
15	74	Freibergs, Lauris	LAT	Honda	14 (7)	15 (6)	13
16	216	Nambotin, Christophe	FRA	Yamaha	18 (3)	13 (8)	11
17	43	Meo, Antoine	FRA	Kawasaki	13 (8)	0	8
18	123	Oddenino, Enrico	ITA	TM	17 (4)	18 (3)	7
19	77	Kovalainen, Marko	FIN	Honda	15 (6)	0	6
20	811	Mossini, Fabio	ITA	Yamaha	0	17 (4)	4
21	21	Dini, Fabrizio	ITA	KTM	0	19 (2)	2
22	34	Noble, James	GBR	Honda	19 (2)	0	2
23	258	Burkhart, Luke	NZL	Suzuki	0	20 (1)	1
24	207	Seronval, Steve	BEL	Yamaha	0	0	0
25	259	Cappelini, Simone	ITA	Yamaha	0	0	0
26	73	Traversini, Thomas	ITA	Aprilia	0	0	0
27	6	Garcia Vico, Francisco	SPA	Aprilia	0	0	0
28	290	Lyons, Adam	IRL	KTM	0	0	0
29	85	Turpin, Vincent	FRA	Honda	0	0	0

MX1 World Championship standings:

Everts 403, Coppins 301, Pichon 294, Melotte 291, Ramon 281, Strijbos 219, Leok 200, Smets 175, Jorgensen 169, de Dijcker 148, Gundersen 133, Atsuta 128, Burnham 123, Garcia Vico 111, Freibergs 107, Seguy 99, Bervoets 97, Noble 92, Kovalainen 79, Theybers 74, Pyrhonen 60, Cooper 42, Meo 37, Bill 36, Martin 31, Oddenino 28, Hucklebridge 25, Nambotin 24, Dobes 23, Demaria 20, Bethys 18, Flockhart 18, Dini 13, Traversini 10, Engwall 10, Dugmore 9, Rose 8, Breugelmans 7, Turpin 7, Robins 5, Beaudouin 4, Mossini 4, Campbell 4, Poikela 3, van den Berg 3, Das 2, Verhoeven 1, Burkhart 1, Lyons 1.

MX2

Overall Position	No.	Rider	Nat.	Bike	Race 1 Pos (Pts)	Race 2 Pos (Pts)	Tot
1	15	McFarlane, Andrew	AUS	Yamaha	1 (25)	1 (25)	50
2	22	Federici, Claudio	ITA	Yamaha	2 (22)	7 (14)	36
3	4	Chiodi, Alessio	ITA	Yamaha	6 (15)	3 (20)	35
4	222	Cairoli, Antonio	ITA	Yamaha	9 (12)	2 (22)	34
5	30	Townley, Ben	NZL	KTM	3 (20)	8 (13)	33
6	37	Caps, Patrick	BEL	Yamaha	5 (16)	6 (15)	31
7	90	Pourcel, Sebastien	FRA	Kawasaki	14 (7)	5 (16)	23
8	87	Dement, Jeff	USA	Honda	10 (11)	9 (12)	23
9	5	Bartolini, Andrea	ITA	Yamaha	8 (13)	11 (10)	23
10	71	Maschio, Mickael	FRA	Kawasaki	0	4 (18)	18
11	19	Sword, Stephen	GBR	Kawasaki	4 (18)	0	18
12	55	Nunn, Carl	GBR	Honda	13 (8)	12 (9)	17
13	38	van Daele, Marvin	BEL	Suzuki	12 (9)	13 (8)	17
14	118	Boissiere, Anthony	FRA	Yamaha	11 (10)	14 (7)	17
15	52	Leuret, Pascal	FRA	KTM	18 (3)	10 (11)	14
16	16	Rattray, Tyla	RSA	KTM	7 (14)	0	14
17	49	Goncalves, Rui	POR	Yamaha	19 (2)	15 (6)	8
18	65	Monni, Manuel	ITA	Yamaha	15 (6)	0	6
19	70	Church, Tom	GBR	Kawasaki	0	16 (5)	5
20	76	Leok, Aigar	EST	KTM	16 (5)	0	5
21	66	Stevanini, Christian	ITA	Honda	0	17 (4)	4
22	95	Nagl, Maximilian	GER	KTM	17 (4)	0	4
23	204	Campano, Carlos	SPA	Yamaha	0	18 (3)	3
24	68	Philippaerts, David	ITA	KTM	0	19 (2)	2
25	121	Salaets, Kristof	BEL	Honda	0	20 (1)	1
26	114	Swanepoel, Garreth	RSA	KTM	20 (1)	0	1
27	69	Avis, Wyatt	RSA	Suzuki	0	0	0
28	46	Guarnieri, Davide	ITA	KTM	0	0	0
29	56	Priem, Manuel	BEL	Suzuki	0	0	0
30	83	Barragan, Jonathan	SPA	KTM	0	0	0

MX2 World Championship standings:

Townley 352, Sword 306, Rattray 291, McFarlane 260, Cairoli 221, Maschio 209, Chiodi 192, Nunn 178, Federici 162, Leok 153, Caps 150, Dobb 142, de Reuver 121, Boissiere 117, Pourcel 111, Philippaerts 103, Dement 88, Barragan 87, van Daele 83, Leuret 81, Priem 75, Bartolini 69, Goncalves 56, Mackenzie 45, Swanepoel 43, Church 40, Nagl 33, Stevanini 32, Narita 30, Monni 28, Cepelak 22, Salaets 20, Guarnieri 10, Cherubini 9, van Vijfeijken 8, Avis 8, Anderson 6, Letellier 6, Aubin 5, Allier 4, Smith 4, Campano 4, Pourcel 3, Barreda 3, Seronval 3, Bernardez 2, Kulhavy 2, Vromans 1.

84

round ten
Grand Prix of Belgium
Neeroeteren, 26-27 June 2004

Grand Prix of Belgium
Neeroeteren, 26-27 June 2004

A Stefan Everts crash is such a rare thing it's hardly surprising that it completely changes a Grand Prix result. Unfortunately for the Belgian, he once again produced a disheartening moment for his home fans after the double moto misery in Zolder at the start of the year. This time his relatively slow spill during the first moto at a rocky Neeroeteren gave Pichon the onus to grab only his second win of the season. The Yamaha had stalled coming into a downhill and Everts was powerless to prevent a flip-flop effect on the gradient. Pichon was aiming to triumph in the Belgian's back yard and was hankering after any small psychological advantage the win might entail. Everts, though, was able to secure the second moto and mount the podium, so any damage was eventually minimal.

The track was a curious beast. Fashioned from a quarry it had no shortage of stones littering the loose and sandy terrain. A lot of work transforming the circuit had taken place and this was widely appreciated, especially by the Belgians. Lots of jumps and twists were overshadowed by two straights of whoops linked by a small turn in the only woodland section. It was among the most technical and difficult obstacles seen on the GP calendar. The Belgian Grand Prix was a crash-strewn weekend. The humps collected several casualties, most notably Melotte and Sword.

Stefan Everts' Belgian residence (he normally lives in Monaco) was a short drive down the road, and the seven-times World Champion used to ride in the nearby woods as a child. Neeroeteren was also a place for numerous title-celebration parties, so the Grand Prix had a special resonance. The Belgian round occurred after a rare free weekend for the riders. The second GP in the country produced

Rattray was exhausting the tape supply but the sore limb did not prevent another GP success.

the usual sights of chips, mayonnaise, beer and lots of replica jerseys and colourful flags.

It was a big weekend for Stephen Sword. The Brit effectively waved goodbye to his World Championship dream after a double salvo of bad luck, failing to score points in either moto due to a crash and mechanical failure. Ben Townley's KTM would also expire into a smoking, rattling mess with the second moto just one lap old to further compound Sword's distress. As per usual, BT managed to win a race before suffering a mishap, keeping his points tally reasonably healthy. Tanel Leok was having his first ride on the Suzuki 450 with the bike in Motovision colours. The Estonian would need time to adapt to the 4-stroke throughout Saturday, but come the MX1 races he was able to slip comfortably into his normal top-ten positions. Joel Smets was back in the paddock watching his machine being handled by another rider, although he was still very weak after being discharged from hospital only a fortnight beforehand. The veteran was now waiting for the course of antibiotics to run its course and the virus to clear for the operation on his knee to go ahead. In the meantime he confessed that he was enjoying some holiday for the first time in his career. Tyla Rattray was keeping a low profile after dislocating his right shoulder while mountain biking with Coppins and Townley during the week. The South African was hiding the handicap but had no problem in explaining the ailment once he had been in the right place at the right time once more to scoop his third MX2 overall win of the season. Teenage US stars Mike and Jeff Alessi were paying a visit to the World Championships and had been in Europe to secretly test the KTM 250. Father and mentor Toni Alessi was impressed by what he saw at Neeroeteren, saying the organisation was better than the AMA series, and identified Strijbos and Townley as the riders that really caught his eye outside of the established set. Cedric Melotte would miss the next two Grand Prix after a fast crash going through the whoops in the first moto. The Belgian could not move for at least ten minutes, during which the riders were slowly funnelled through the section. Leaving the circuit in an ambulance, a suspected broken femur was later diagnosed as a nasty dislocated hip. Javier Garcia Vico and Aprilia mutually parted ways prior to Neeroeteren. The Spaniard wanted a more competitive machine while the Italians emphasised the priority of development. Vico, the 2003 650cc runner-up, would not contest another Grand Prix in 2004.

Likeable Spaniard Javier Garcia Vico was no longer a GP rider after splitting with the struggling Aprilia.

Above: Maschio came close once again but a last-minute error produced another low.

Right: Jeff Dement gave Honda their first MX2 podium result.

Opposite Page: Townley brushed aside McFarlane's challenge but the KTM didn't fancy the second moto in Belgium.

motocross
2004 Grand Prix Review

Pichon was looking to gain a psychological advantage in Everts' back yard. It almost worked.

A busy day for the MX2 Champion KTM team and Townley's mechanic especially.

Saturday

Another sunny day, another Mickael Pichon pole. The eighth fastest time of the season for the Honda rider was excellent work, considering he had never ridden the circuit before. The former American Supercross Champion liked the technical demands of the course and beat both Everts and Strijbos with a flying lap deep into the thirty-minute chrono. Everts was relaxed with second place and even had time to joke: 'Every weekend is the same. If I set a pole time then Mickael goes straight out and tries to beat me. But I don't mind. Let him win on Saturday and I can win on Sunday.' Not everyone was finding the circuit an easy test. Strijbos was a second slower in third while Jorgensen was almost another second further back in fourth. Ramon was just ahead of Coppins, and the KTM rider was trying to jump out of a patchy mid-season spell of form, with podium results slipping away thanks to basic errors.

All seemed well for Stephen Sword on Saturday evening. The Kawasaki rider had set the second-fastest time behind Townley in pre-qualifying and then holeshotted the second-heat race to win by six seconds and without hassle from teammate Maschio. Rattray was a conservative third in front of American Jeff Dement. Christophe Pourcel had learned from the French GP and guided his 125cc Kawasaki to eleventh, leading Tom Church and trailing Max Nagl. Ben

Townley owned the first heat for his eighth qualifying victory of the campaign. The Kiwi defeated McFarlane (although the pair would clash more controversially on Sunday) and Pourcel with Cairoli and Aigar Leok lingering in the lower top five.

Sunday

'Ben rode aggressively in the first moto and made a very forceful move. We go to Sweden next and I will train hard and be looking to pay that back.' A scent of resentment and rivalry between McFarlane and Townley began to spring up after the collision. The pair certainly weren't friends. The KTM rider had allegedly jumped into McFarlane on the second lap while scrapping for positions just behind holeshotter Cairoli. The result was a Yamaha with a broken wheel and McFarlane screamed through the pits extra-agitated when the team could not fix the problem as fast as he liked. He eventually decided to retire after two laps far behind the pack. Townley passed Cairoli within two circulations and faced some gutsy pressure from Pourcel until the teenager stalled the Kawasaki. Sword was in second place for a lap until he hit neutral going through the whoops and flipped over the bars. Sore and winded, he could not restart. Rattray found himself elevated to second with Pourcel fighting off Dement on the Honda after the American had made a positive start.

If Townley was at fault for McFarlane's DNF then he paid for his crime in the second race when the KTM prototype boiled over within two laps. It was the first mechanical failure for number 30 but would not be the last. New leader McFarlane must have grinned passing the pits and seeing the steam rising out of the KTM box, but was not given the race on a plate as Maschio swiftly moved ahead. After ten laps at the front, the Frenchman suffered a problem with his rear brake and then crashed in the very last seconds to allow McFarlane through for his third moto victory from the last four. Maschio's blunder lost him the 'overall' as Rattray's fourth place behind Dement helped him towards a higher point total. Sword had been in some pain but a top-ten result evaporated on lap five when the Kawasaki broke.

It was a different top three entirely for round ten, with none of Italy's 'podiumees' able to get close at Neeroeteren. Pourcel missed out on a debut celebration due to an awful start as Dement happily collected his first trophy for four years, and was also surprisingly the first rider to give the Honda 250 its maiden rostrum appearance.

Mickael Pichon was free to win by seven seconds over his teammate in the first moto after Everts had crashed on lap five while trying to detach himself from the attentions of Jorgensen. The crowd were startled by the image of their hero on the ground but happily cheered him back to a distant sixth position which would help enormously towards his eventual podium reward. Melotte had passed Strijbos for third before his big crash on the same lap. Ramon was then searching for a way to overtake Strijbos but before he knew it, Coppins caught and relegated the Belgian to fifth. Ramon was then regularly checking over his shoulder to monitor the progress of the closing Everts.

The World Champion was out for revenge against lady luck in the second moto and dragged Pichon with him when he overtook holeshotter Strijbos on the third lap. Kevin was a jaded figure compared to the yellow blur in Italy. As in the second Italian moto Everts was happy to play follow-my-leader with Pichon, with the Frenchman doing all he could in the first two-thirds to force his rival into his roost. Wisely he backed off slightly in the closing stages, well aware the overall triumph was all his. Ramon and Coppins both passed Strijbos and this time Ramon remained strong to gain his third podium for KTM, immensely satisfied with the bottom step at his home GP. Jorgensen demonstrated the extremely thin difference between a good and bad start when he could only take eighth, although the Dane was still looking for race fitness.

Joel Smets was back at a Grand Prix but was still in a weakened condition after his bacterial infection.

Townley had to watch fifteen points being slashed from his championship margin by 'Ratters' (as he affectionately calls him) but with a difference of forty-six intact there was no need for panic. If anybody was sweating it was Sword, who lost a lot of ground and saw the distance to runner-up spot extend to a moto (twenty-five points).

Four points in front of Coppins, Pichon was now Everts' closest challenger but the champion's refusal to have a disastrous weekend meant that the 102-point gap to the leader was looking like a colossal quantity. Zolder aside, Everts had been solidly mounting performances and podiums and was now, with a two Grand Prix cushion, in a position to start counting down the motos.

motocross
2004 Grand Prix Review

MX1

Overall Position	No.	Rider	Nat.	Bike	Race 1 Pos (Pts)	Race 2 Pos (Pts)	Total
1	2	Pichon, Mickael	FRA	Honda	1 (25)	2 (22)	47
2	72	Everts, Stefan	BEL	Yamaha	6 (15)	1 (25)	40
3	11	Ramon, Steve	BEL	KTM	5 (16)	3 (20)	36
4	31	Coppins, Joshua	NZL	Honda	4 (18)	4 (18)	36
5	24	Strijbos, Kevin	BEL	Suzuki	3 (20)	5 (16)	36
6	8	Jorgensen, Brian	DEN	Honda	2 (22)	8 (13)	35
7	28	Seguy, Luigi	FRA	Yamaha	8 (13)	6 (15)	28
8	40	Leok, Tanel	EST	Suzuki	7 (14)	7 (14)	28
9	97	Breugelmans, Sven	BEL	KTM	9 (12)	13 (8)	20
10	105	Bill, Julien	SUI	KTM	14 (7)	10 (11)	18
11	74	Freibergs, Lauris	LAT	Honda	10 (11)	14 (7)	18
12	48	Burnham, Christian	GBR	KTM	11 (10)	15 (6)	16
13	75	Dobes, Josef	CZE	Suzuki	15 (6)	12 (9)	15
14	80	de Dijcker, Ken	BEL	Honda	0	9 (12)	12
15	34	Noble, James	GBR	Honda	19 (2)	11 (10)	12
16	77	Kovalainen, Marko	FIN	Honda	12 (9)	18 (3)	12
17	12	Theybers, Danny	BEL	Yamaha	16 (5)	16 (5)	10
18	21	Dini, Fabrizio	ITA	KTM	17 (4)	17 (4)	8
19	50	Hucklebridge, Mark	GBR	KTM	13 (8)	0	8
20	200	Godrie, Christof	BEL	Honda	20 (1)	19 (2)	3
21	123	Oddenino, Enrico	ITA	TM	18 (3)	0	3
22	27	Atsuta, Yoshitaka	JPN	Honda	0	20 (1)	1
23	237	Boller, Andreas	GER	Honda	0	0	0
24	261	Beconini, Manuel	ITA	Yamaha	0	0	0
25	260	Segers, David	BEL	Yamaha	0	0	0
26	73	Traversini, Thomas	ITA	Aprilia	0	0	0
27	207	Seronval, Steve	BEL	Yamaha	0	0	0
28	7	Melotte, Cedric	BEL	Yamaha	0	0	0
29	258	Burkhart, Luke	NZL	Suzuki	0	0	0

MX1 World Championship standings:

Everts 443, Pichon 341, Coppins 337, Ramon 317, Melotte 291, Strijbos 255, Leok 228, Jorgensen 204, Smets 175, de Dijcker 160, Burnham 139, Gundersen 133, Atsuta 129, Seguy 127, Freibergs 125, Garcia Vico 111, Noble 104, Bervoets 97, Kovalainen 91, Theybers 84, Pyrhonen 60, Bill 54, Cooper 42, Dobes 38, Meo 37, Hucklebridge 33, Martin 31, Oddenino 31, Breugelmans 27, Nambotin 24, Dini 21, Demaria 20, Bethys 18, Flockhart 18, Traversini 10, Engwall 10, Dugmore 9, Rose 8, Turpin 7, Robins 5, Beaudouin 4, Mossini 4, Campbell 4, Poikela 3, van den Berg 3, Godrie 3, Das 2, Verhoeven ,1 Lyons 1, Burkhart 1.

MX2

Overall Position	No.	Rider	Nat.	Bike	Race 1 Pos (Pts)	Race 2 Pos (Pts)	Total
1	16	Rattray, Tyla	RSA	KTM	2 (22)	4 (18)	40
2	71	Maschio, Mickael	FRA	Kawasaki	5 (16)	2 (22)	38
3	87	Dement, Jeff	USA	Honda	4 (18)	3 (20)	38
4	90	Pourcel, Sebastien	FRA	Kawasaki	3 (20)	6 (15)	35
5	37	Caps, Patrick	BEL	Yamaha	6 (15)	5 (16)	31
6	15	McFarlane, Andrew	AUS	Yamaha	0	1 (25)	25
7	30	Townley, Ben	NZL	KTM	1 (25)	0	25
8	38	van Daele, Marvin	BEL	Suzuki	11 (10)	9 (12)	22
9	4	Chiodi, Alessio	ITA	Yamaha	14 (7)	11 (10)	17
10	56	Priem, Manuel	BEL	Suzuki	18 (3)	8 (13)	16
11	66	Stevanini, Christian	ITA	Honda	8 (13)	18 (3)	16
12	49	Goncalves, Rui	POR	Yamaha	17 (4)	10 (11)	15
13	222	Cairoli, Antonio	ITA	Yamaha	0	7 (14)	14
14	263	Seistola, Matti	FIN	Honda	16 (5)	12 (9)	14
15	76	Leok, Aigar	EST	KTM	7 (14)	0	14
16	95	Nagl, Maximilian	GER	KTM	13 (8)	16 (5)	13
17	55	Nunn, Carl	GBR	Honda	10 (11)	19 (2)	13
18	118	Boissiere, Anthony	FRA	Yamaha	15 (6)	15 (6)	12
19	64	Dobb, James	GBR	Honda	9 (12)	0	12
20	68	Philippaerts, David	ITA	KTM	12 (9)	0	9
21	65	Monni, Manuel	ITA	Yamaha	0	13 (8)	8
22	83	Barragan, Jonathan	SPA	KTM	0	14 (7)	7
23	377	Pourcel, Christophe	FRA	Kawasaki	19 (2)	17 (4)	6
24	114	Swanepoel, Garreth	RSA	KTM	0	20 (1)	1
25	70	Church, Tom	GBR	Kawasaki	20 (1)	0	1
26	22	Federici, Claudio	ITA	Yamaha	0	0	0
27	19	Sword, Stephen	GBR	Kawasaki	0	0	0
28	82	Tarroux, Jeremy	FRA	Suzuki	0	0	0
29	5	Bartolini, Andrea	ITA	Yamaha	0	0	0
30	711	Allier, Tomas	FRA	Kawasaki	0	0	0
31	52	Leuret, Pascal	FRA	KTM	0	0	0
32	46	Guarnieri, Davide	ITA	KTM	0	0	0

MX2 World Championship standings:

Townley 377, Rattray 331, Sword 306, McFarlane 285, Maschio 247, Cairoli 235, Chiodi 209, Nunn 191, Caps 181, Leok 167, Federici 162, Dobb 154, Pourcel 146, Boissiere 129, Dement 126, de Reuver 121, Philippaerts 112, van Daele 105, Barragan 94, Priem 91, Leuret 81, Goncalves 71, Bartolini 69, Stevanini 48, Nagl 46, Mackenzie 45, Swanepoel 44, Church 41, Monni 36, Narita 30, Cepelak 22, Salaets 20, Seistola 14, Guarnieri 10, Cherubini 9, Pourcel 9, van Vijfeijken 8, Avis 8, Letellier 6, Anderson 6, Aubin 5, Allier 4, Smith 4, Campano 4, Barreda 3, Seronval 3, Bernardez 2, Kulhavy 2, Vromans 1.

round eleven
Grand Prix of Sweden
Uddevalla, 3-4 July 2004

motocross
2004 Grand Prix Review

MX1

Overall Position	No.	Rider	Nat.	Bike	Race 1 Pos (Pts)	Race 2 Pos (Pts)	Total
1	2	**Pichon, Mickael**	FRA	Honda	3 (20)	1 (25)	45
2	8	**Jorgensen, Brian**	DEN	Honda	2 (22)	3 (20)	42
3	72	**Everts, Stefan**	BEL	Yamaha	4 (18)	2 (22)	40
4	24	**Strijbos, Kevin**	BEL	Suzuki	1 (25)	6 (15)	40
5	11	**Ramon, Steve**	BEL	KTM	6 (15)	4 (18)	33
6	77	**Kovalainen, Marko**	FIN	Honda	8 (13)	10 (11)	24
7	26	**Pyrhonen, Antti**	FIN	TM	5 (16)	13 (8)	24
8	31	**Coppins, Joshua**	NZL	Honda	13 (8)	9 (12)	20
9	111	**Eliasson, Joakim**	SWE	Honda	16 (5)	8 (13)	18
10	27	**Atsuta, Yoshitaka**	JPN	Honda	0	5 (16)	16
11	21	Dini, Fabrizio	ITA	KTM	15 (6)	12 (9)	15
12	40	Leok, Tanel	EST	Suzuki	0	7 (14)	14
13	50	Hucklebridge, Mark	GBR	KTM	17 (4)	11 (10)	14
14	123	Oddenino, Enrico	ITA	TM	10 (11)	18 (3)	14
15	80	de Dijcker, Ken	BEL	Honda	7 (14)	0	14
16	97	Breugelmans, Sven	BEL	KTM	9 (12)	0	12
17	74	Freibergs, Lauris	LAT	Honda	18 (3)	14 (7)	10
18	28	Seguy, Luigi	FRA	Yamaha	11 (10)	0	10
19	88	Laansoo, Juss	EST	Honda	12 (9)	0	9
20	12	Theybers, Danny	BEL	Yamaha	20 (1)	15 (6)	7
21	75	Dobes, Josef	CZE	Suzuki	14 (7)	0	7
22	48	Burnham, Christian	GBR	KTM	19 (2)	17 (4)	6
23	34	Noble, James	GBR	Honda	0	16 (5)	5
24	268	Nilsson, Mats	SWE	Yamaha	0	19 (2)	2
25	79	Lindhe, Jonny	SWE	Honda	0	20 (1)	1
26	73	Traversini, Thomas	ITA	Aprilia	0	0	0
27	267	Karlsson, Frederik	SWE	Husqvarna	0	0	0
28	284	Vangsbakken, Kristen	NOR	Yamaha	0	0	0
29	261	Beconini, Manuel	ITA	Yamaha	0	0	0
30	42	Karlsson, Joakim	SWE	Yamaha	0	0	0

MX1 World Championship standings:

Everts 483, Pichon 386, Coppins 357, Ramon 350, Strijbos 295, Melotte 291, Jorgensen 246, Leok 242, Smets 175, de Dijcker 174, Atsuta 145, Burnham 145, Seguy 137, Freibergs 135, Gundersen 133, Kovalainen 115, Garcia Vico 111, Noble 109, Bervoets 97, Theybers 91, Pyrhonen 84, Bill 54, Hucklebridge 47, Oddenino 45, Dobes 45, Cooper 42, Breugelmans 39, Meo 37, Dini 36, Martin 31, Nambotin 24, Demaria 20, Eliasson 18, Bethys 18, Flockhart 18, Traversini 10, Engwall 10, Dugmore 9, Laansoo 9, Rose 8, Turpin 7, Robins 5, Beaudouin 4, Mossini 4, Campbell 4, Poikela 3, van den Berg 3, Godrie 3, Das 2, Nilsson 2, Verhoeven 1, Burkhart 1, Lyons 1, Lindhe 1.

MX2

Overall Position	No.	Rider	Nat.	Bike	Race 1 Pos (Pts)	Race 2 Pos (Pts)	Total
1	30	**Townley, Ben**	NZL	KTM	1 (25)	1 (25)	50
2	4	**Chiodi, Alessio**	ITA	Yamaha	2 (22)	2 (22)	44
3	5	**Bartolini, Andrea**	ITA	Yamaha	3 (20)	4 (18)	38
4	19	**Sword, Stephen**	GBR	Kawasaki	5 (16)	3 (20)	36
5	37	**Caps, Patrick**	BEL	Yamaha	4 (18)	6 (15)	33
6	87	**Dement, Jeff**	USA	Honda	8 (13)	10 (11)	24
7	222	**Cairoli, Antonio**	ITA	Yamaha	15 (6)	5 (16)	22
8	16	**Rattray, Tyla**	RSA	KTM	12 (9)	11 (10)	19
9	52	**Leuret, Pascal**	FRA	KTM	11 (10)	12 (9)	19
10	118	**Boissiere, Anthony**	FRA	Yamaha	9 (12)	14 (7)	19
11	55	Nunn, Carl	GBR	Honda	10 (11)	15 (6)	17
12	49	Goncalves, Rui	POR	Yamaha	13 (8)	13 (8)	16
13	15	McFarlane, Andrew	AUS	Yamaha	6 (15)	0	15
14	71	Maschio, Mickael	FRA	Kawasaki	0	7 (14)	14
15	69	Avis, Wyatt	RSA	Suzuki	19 (2)	9 (12)	14
16	22	Federici, Claudio	ITA	Yamaha	7 (14)	0	14
17	56	Priem, Manuel	BEL	Suzuki	0	8 (13)	13
18	114	Swanepoel, Garreth	RSA	KTM	18 (3)	16 (5)	8
19	68	Philippaerts, David	ITA	KTM	17 (4)	18 (3)	7
20	65	Monni, Manuel	ITA	Yamaha	16 (5)	19 (2)	7
21	281	Pirinen, Jukka	FIN	Honda	14 (7)	0	7
22	76	Leok, Aigar	EST	KTM	0	17 (4)	4
23	377	Pourcel, Christophe	FRA	Kawasaki	0	20 (1)	1
24	38	van Daele, Marvin	BEL	Suzuki	20 (1)	0	1
25	82	Tarroux, Jeremy	FRA	Suzuki	0	0	0
26	273	Carlsson, Johan	SWE	Yamaha	0	0	0
27	263	Seistola, Matti	FIN	Honda	0	0	0
28	66	Stevanini, Christian	ITA	Honda	0	0	0
29	711	Allier, Tomas	FRA	Kawasaki	0	0	0
30	90	Pourcel, Sebastien	FRA	Kawasaki	0	0	0
31	103	Andersson, Stefan	SWE	Husaberg	0	0	0

MX2 World Championship standings:

Townley 427, Rattray 350, Sword 342, McFarlane 300, Maschio 261, Cairoli 257, Chiodi 253, Caps 214, Nunn 208, Federici 176, Leok 171, Dobb 154, Dement 150, Boissiere 148, Pourcel 146, de Reuver 121, Philippaerts 119, Bartolini 107, van Daele 106, Priem 104, Leuret 100, Barragan 94, Goncalves 87, Swanepoel 52, Stevanini 48, Nagl 46, Mackenzie 45, Monni 43, Church 41, Narita 30, Cepelak 22, Avis 22, Salaets 20, Seistola 14, Guarnieri 10, Pourcel 10, Cherubini 9, van Vijfeijken 8, Pirinen 7, Anderson 6, Letellier 6, Aubin 5, Allier 4, Smith 4, Campano 4, Barreda 3, Seronval 3, Bernardez 2, Kulhavy 2, Vromans 1.

Grand Prix of the Czech Republic

Loket, 31 July -1 August 2004

motocross
2004 Grand Prix Review

MX1

Overall Position	No.	Rider	Nat.	Bike	Race 1 Pos (Pts)	Race 2 Pos (Pts)	Total
1	2	**Pichon, Mickael**	FRA	Honda	1 (25)	1 (25)	50
2	72	**Everts, Stefan**	BEL	Yamaha	2 (22)	2 (22)	44
3	31	**Coppins, Joshua**	NZL	Honda	3 (20)	3 (20)	40
4	24	**Strijbos, Kevin**	BEL	Suzuki	7 (14)	4 (18)	32
5	8	**Jorgensen, Brian**	DEN	Honda	4 (18)	7 (14)	32
6	40	**Leok, Tanel**	EST	Suzuki	5 (16)	6 (15)	31
7	28	**Seguy, Luigi**	FRA	Yamaha	8 (13)	5 (16)	29
8	11	**Ramon, Steve**	BEL	KTM	6 (15)	12 (9)	24
9	48	**Burnham, Christian**	GBR	KTM	10 (11)	10 (11)	22
10	80	**de Dijcker, Ken**	BEL	Honda	13 (8)	8 (13)	21
11	105	Bill, Julien	SUI	KTM	11 (10)	15 (6)	16
12	27	Atsuta, Yoshitaka	JPN	Honda	0	9 (12)	12
13	97	Breugelmans, Sven	BEL	KTM	9 (12)	0	12
14	117	Jones, Mark	GBR	KTM	0	11 (10)	10
15	74	Freibergs, Lauris	LAT	Honda	18 (3)	14 (7)	10
16	18	Bervoets, Marnicq	BEL	Yamaha	12 (9)	0	9
17	34	Noble, James	GBR	Honda	0	13 (8)	8
18	77	Kovalainen, Marko	FIN	Honda	17 (4)	17 (4)	8
19	89	Zerava, Martin	CZE	KTM	14 (7)	0	7
20	12	Theybers, Danny	BEL	Yamaha	15 (6)	0	6
21	43	Meo, Antoine	FRA	Kawasaki	0	16 (5)	5
22	26	Pyrhonen, Antti	FIN	TM	16 (5)	0	5
23	75	Dobes, Josef	CZE	Suzuki	0	18 (3)	3
24	287	Kucirek, Miroslav	CZE	Honda	19 (2)	20 (1)	3
25	123	Oddenino, Enrico	ITA	TM	0	19 (2)	2
26	54	Beggi, Cristian	ITA	Honda	20 (1)	0	1
27	61	Kragelj, Saso	SLO	Yamaha	0	0	0
28	288	Izoird, Fabien	FRA	Suzuki	0	0	0
29	73	Traversini, Thomas	ITA	Aprilia	0	0	0
30	20	Jelen, Roman	SLO	Husqvarna	0	0	0

MX1 World Championship standings:

Everts 527, Pichon 436, Coppins 397, Ramon 374, Strijbos 327, Melotte 291, Jorgensen 278, Leok 273, de Dijcker 195, Smets 175, Burnham 167, Seguy 166, Atsuta 157, Freibergs 145, Gundersen 133, Kovalainen 123, Noble 117, Garcia Vico 111, Bervoets 106, Theybers 97, Pyrhonen 89, Bill 70, Breugelmans 51, Dobes 48, Oddenino 47, Huckebridge 47, Cooper 42, Meo 42, Dini 36, Martin 31, Nambotin 24, Demaria 20, Eliasson 18, Bethys 18, Flockhart 18, Jones 10, Traversini 10, Engwall 10, Dugmore 9, Laansoo 9, Rose 8, Zerava ,7 Turpin 7, Robins 5, Beaudouin 4, Mossini 4, Campbell 4, Poikela 3, Kucirek 3, Godrie 3, van den Berg 3, Das 2, Nilsson 2, Verhoeven 1, Lyons 1, Burkhart 1, Beggi 1, Lindhe 1.

MX2

Overall Position	No.	Rider	Nat.	Bike	Race 1 Pos (Pts)	Race 2 Pos (Pts)	Tot
1	30	**Townley, Ben**	NZL	KTM	3 (20)	1 (25)	45
2	4	**Chiodi, Alessio**	ITA	Yamaha	4 (18)	2 (22)	40
3	222	**Cairoli, Antonio**	ITA	Yamaha	1 (25)	6 (15)	40
4	17	**de Reuver, Marc**	NED	KTM	2 (22)	9 (12)	34
5	16	**Rattray, Tyla**	RSA	KTM	11 (10)	4 (18)	28
6	5	**Bartolini, Andrea**	ITA	Yamaha	6 (15)	8 (13)	28
7	22	**Federici, Claudio**	ITA	Yamaha	7 (14)	12 (9)	23
8	71	**Maschio, Mickael**	FRA	Kawasaki	13 (8)	7 (14)	22
9	118	**Boissiere, Anthony**	FRA	Yamaha	9 (12)	11 (10)	22
10	90	**Pourcel, Sebastien**	FRA	Kawasaki	0	3 (20)	20
11	55	Nunn, Carl	GBR	Honda	17 (4)	5 (16)	20
12	19	Sword, Stephen	GBR	Kawasaki	8 (13)	15 (6)	19
13	37	Caps, Patrick	BEL	Yamaha	5 (16)	0	16
14	83	Barragan, Jonathan	SPA	KTM	14 (7)	13 (8)	15
15	269	Vehvilainen, Jussi	FIN	Honda	10 (11)	17 (4)	15
16	49	Goncalves, Rui	POR	Yamaha	18 (3)	10 (11)	14
17	114	Swanepoel, Garreth	RSA	KTM	15 (6)	14 (7)	13
18	377	Pourcel, Christophe	FRA	Kawasaki	12 (9)	0	9
19	52	Leuret, Pascal	FRA	KTM	0	16 (5)	5
20	76	Leok, Aigar	EST	KTM	16 (5)	0	5
21	65	Monni, Manuel	ITA	Yamaha	0	18 (3)	3
22	95	Nagl, Maximilian	GER	KTM	19 (2)	20 (1)	3
23	263	Seistola, Matti	FIN	Honda	0	19 (2)	2
24	251	Aubin, Nicolas	FRA	Kawasaki	20 (1)	0	1
25	38	van Daele, Marvin	BEL	Suzuki	0	0	0
26	69	Avis, Wyatt	RSA	Suzuki	0	0	0
27	68	Philippaerts, David	ITA	KTM	0	0	0
28	66	Stevanini, Christian	ITA	Honda	0	0	0
29	92	Cherubini, Luca	ITA	Suzuki	0	0	0
30	121	Salaets, Kristof	BEL	Honda	0	0	0
31	87	Dement, Jeff	USA	Honda	0	0	0

MX2 World Championship standings:

Townley 472, Rattray 378, Sword 361, McFarlane 300, Cairoli 297, Chiodi 293, Maschio 283, Caps 230, Nunn 228, Federici 199, Leok 176, Boissiere 170, Pourcel 166, de Reuver 155, Dobb 154, Dement 150, Bartolini 135, Philippaerts 119, Barragan 109, van Daele 106, Leuret 105, Priem 104, Goncalves 101, Swanepoel 65, Nagl 49, Stevanini 48, Monni 46, Mackenzie 45, Church 41, Narita 30, Cepelak 22, Avis 22, Salaets 20, Pourcel 19, Seistola 16, Vehvilainen 15, Guarnieri 10, Cherubini 9, van Vijfeijken 8, Pirinen 7, Anderson 6, Letellier 6, Aubin 6, Allier 4, Smith 4, Campano 4, Barreda 3, Seronval 3, Bernardez 2, Kulhavy 2, Vromans 1.

round thirteen
Grand Prix of Wallonie
Namur, 7-8 August 2004

when he dropped a bombshell on his Yamaha UK team by announcing that he had signed for the Italian Errezeta squad to replace the retiring Andrea Bartolini for 2005. Tanel Leok had also confirmed a factory Kawasaki contract for the following year, regrettably turning down a smaller offer from Motovision. Youthstream were also looking to obtain signatures by pushing the teams into a contract for the 2005 World Championship, but there were several contentious points that prevented a flood of paperwork arriving back to the YS hospitality HQ. Prize money, expenses and a selective entry list aside, the deliberation also concerned the promoters' wish to make the teams responsible for their riders; in effect asking the teams to cast a tight leash on their track stars in terms of outside race appearances and making them liable for penalties if everyone didn't play ball. Rumours in Namur of a possible breakaway series caused some alarm and Youthstream, together with the FIM, held a press conference on Sunday to state that they didn't recognise the point of MXTAG and would not grant an audience to the representative body. Giuseppe Luongo stated that he had personal dialogue with the teams but the fact remained that many had still not signed the contract and a majority were putting their faith in TAG to see what they could achieve if a spot at the negotiating table was ever an eventuality. TAG had held a meeting on Friday and somehow also had an informal chat with Youthstream over the weekend. The sticking points of the contract were hot issues and further developments would occur at the Grand Prix of Europe. In the following weeks Luongo was in fact communicating with Valat, and indeed justifying parts of the contract, but it seemed that an agreement was highly unlikely. Valat, however, was quietly doing good work by getting the teams' objections and concerns heard.

Saturday

Pichon racked a seventh consecutive pole and it was clear that nobody else was going to get a look-in for the rest of the season in Timed Practice. The Frenchman is not a fan of the track but, like most, enjoys the atmosphere and the occasion. Everts had been fastest in free practice, but Pichon fiddled with the Honda's suspension again and his last lap of seven in the chrono was a second faster than Coppins, with Everts close-by in third. Suzuki duo Strijbos and Leok were fourth and fifth.

Tyla Rattray suffered a sickening crash in the second MX2 qualifying heat. Rising the large jump that threw the riders off the Esplanade and into the woods, he tangled with Stevanini's rider-less machine and fell a long way into the shade.

Hunched over the bars, new dad Everts thunders past the café.

The ambulance was called and the South African was carried away but the overreaction was quelled when he was soon back on his feet, having banged the shoulder he dislocated several weeks before. Rattray grimaced his way through the Last Chance session and finished fifth to at least be a part of the GP before rushing to get as much attention and physio to the joint as possible. Townley won the heat from Pourcel and the weakened Sword with McFarlane in fourth. Marc de Reuver had been second but dropped back to eighth after his fork clip (to grasp the suspension at the start) broke and depressed the front end, causing him to slow before the plastic lip finally snapped away, allowing him to finish the twenty-five-minute sprint. Alessio Chiodi won a close first race from Caps and Federici, beating Maschio to third spot. Vehvilainen was fifth and come Sunday morning would use the distinct advantage of a strong start at Namur to devastating effect.

The dark arrived and the rain closed play, coming down with real force and soaking the track to its core. The terrain would now be a playground for the 4-strokes on Sunday, but the bad weather was timed appropriately because the sunshine was back twelve hours later.

Sunday

In front of an expectant crowd for the last Benelux race of the year Steve Ramon holeshotted and led a chaotic first lap as the 450s crammed around the narrow course. Jorgensen crashed in front of the pack coming out of the whoops and didn't continue due to an injured leg. He scooped up Yves Demaria, making another MX1 outing, but the big Frenchman also pulled out with a hurt finger. Cedric Melotte lasted five laps before his back pain was too much to take. Everts had debunked Ramon with Pichon and Coppins charging through by the second lap. Pichon crashed at the steep drop-down and lost six positions needing to re-fire the Honda. He was able to recover to fourth but the error had given Coppins

Kevin Strijbos poses in front of a typical Namur background. The Belgian was to straighten up and head into the woods.

Tanel Leok gazes out from the Motovision confines but the factory Kawasaki rig is not too far into the distance.

Brian Jorgensen unknowingly prepares for his last GP appearance of the year and also as a Honda rider, having signed a contract with Yamaha for 2005.

and Ramon the rest of the top-three positions seven seconds behind Everts. Billy Mackenzie collected an impressive tenth position on the Yamaha UK 450 after swapping classes, while Ken de Dijcker and Juilen Bill also breached the leaderboard.

Everts led the first lap of the second moto but a momentary slip, illustrating perfectly the thinner line than usual between winning and losing at Namur, allowed Pichon through to take the race. Everts found himself with Ramon for company and the duo passed Strijbos to move up the order. Coppins had broken free in second and would record results of 2-2, to again walk away with a trophy. Ramon crashed in big style on lap seven trying to pass Everts for third and was lucky not to be hurt as he flipped into the trees. Jorgensen made a cleaner start and was fifth behind Strijbos. Danny Theybers, Marnicq Bervoets and Josef Dobes filled top-ten positions and their highest results of the season. The MX1 motos were exciting in brief passing spells but the time gaps between the riders showed that the real racing was against the track rather than other participants. Everts would claim the Grand Prix by one point from Coppins.

Another completely different podium lineup for the MX2 class appeared in front of the colourful crowd as the factory KTMs didn't seem to like the punishing trek through the Namur circuit. Fans were treated to a vision of what a 'Townley-de

'Reuver-free' race would look like. Vehvilainen spearheaded the pack into the fast first turn and led a tight double of Chiodi and the surprisingly fast Cairoli for the opening nine laps until he almost crashed and dropped back to seventh in front of Rattray. 'Chicco' gratefully accepted the lead and won his first moto since 1999. Maschio was elevated to third. Townley had started poorly and took half the race to find a spot to pass Caps for sixth before the KTM developed a fuel leak and he registered his fifth DNF of the season. De Reuver followed two laps later while also in sixth place, this time with gearbox trouble. Vehvilainen was at it again in the second moto but Townley was understandably fired-up and more aggressive, taking four positions in five laps to seize the lead. De Reuver followed and assumed the runner-up place at the halfway stage. McFarlane had been fourth but was suffering with his shoulder and ebbed back to eighth; it was still enough to deliver a surprise podium. Sword had a strong second moto to keep some hope of catching Rattray for the number-two plate. Cairoli was fourth behind Vehvilainen, who found some reserves to score his first overall top three since 2001. 'This is like a dream,' he said, adopting the common emotion of the weekend. 'Today was only my second GP since Moscow 2002 and to get on the podium here, especially in Namur, is great for me. I spent a lot of time away from the sport. I had a three-month break to recover and have been training for six weeks and things are getting better every day.' Cairoli was also ecstatic for different reasons. 'When I arrived here yesterday I had some problems to understand the track and to find a good rhythm but lap after lap it was better and better,' said the winner. 'At the end of the day things were going well and I started to enjoy it.'

The remaining races were slipping by fast and the timing of Namur for Everts was crucial in ending Pichon's mini-fightback. The two points gained were less important than the fact that none were lost by Everts in Belgium. With a lead of 93 and just 150 left to win, title number eight was within mathematical reach. Townley was again able to rescue something from a disastrous GP and was blessed by the fact that Rattray could only finish fourth overall and chip his Championship lead by a single point.

The last word had to go to the 'daddy' of them all, Stefan Everts, 'Mr' Namur: 'I think that this weekend has been the most emotional in my life! Friday has been a great day for me and then winning in Namur is a dream come true. In both races I was really aggressive from the beginning, like Mickael was in Czech Republic. The track was this year really physical, it was very hot and it was hard in some places to stay focused.'

Pichon celebrates a second moto win and third place overall after an exhausting day's racing at Namur.

motocross
2004 Grand Prix Review

MX1

Overall Position	No.	Rider	Nat.	Bike	Race 1 Pos (Pts)	Race 2 Pos (Pts)	Total
1	72	Everts, Stefan	BEL	Yamaha	1 (25)	3 (20)	45
2	31	Coppins, Joshua	NZL	Honda	2 (22)	2 (22)	44
3	2	Pichon, Mickael	FRA	Honda	4 (18)	1 (25)	43
4	24	Strijbos, Kevin	BEL	Suzuki	6 (15)	4 (18)	33
5	40	Leok, Tanel	EST	Suzuki	11 (10)	6 (15)	25
6	27	Atsuta, Yoshitaka	JPN	Honda	8 (13)	10 (11)	24
7	75	Dobes, Josef	CZE	Suzuki	12 (9)	9 (12)	21
8	11	Ramon, Steve	BEL	KTM	3 (20)	0	20
9	8	Jorgensen, Brian	DEN	Honda	0	5 (16)	16
10	77	Kovalainen, Marko	FIN	Honda	14 (7)	12 (9)	16
11	80	de Dijcker, Ken	BEL	Honda	5 (16)	0	16
12	105	Bill, Julien	SUI	KTM	7 (14)	20 (1)	15
13	12	Theybers, Danny	BEL	Yamaha	0	7 (14)	14
14	18	Bervoets, Marnicq	BEL	Yamaha	0	8 (13)	13
15	21	Dini, Fabrizio	ITA	KTM	15 (6)	14 (7)	13
16	74	Freibergs, Lauris	LAT	Honda	17 (4)	13 (8)	12
17	28	Seguy, Luigi	FRA	Yamaha	9 (12)	0	12
18	34	Noble, James	GBR	Honda	20 (1)	11 (10)	11
19	211	Mackenzie, Billy	GBR	Yamaha	10 (11)	0	11
20	26	Pyrhonen, Antti	FIN	TM	16 (5)	17 (4)	9
21	48	Burnham, Christian	GBR	KTM	13 (8)	0	8
22	117	Jones, Mark	GBR	KTM	0	15 (6)	6
23	97	Breugelmans, Sven	BEL	KTM	0	16 (5)	5
24	288	Izoird, Fabien	FRA	Suzuki	0	18 (3)	3
25	123	Oddenino, Enrico	ITA	TM	18 (3)	0	3
26	43	Meo, Antoine	FRA	Kawasaki	0	19 (2)	2
27	200	Godrie, Christof	BEL	Honda	19 (2)	0	2
28	296	Vanderheyden, Wim	BEL	Yamaha	0	0	0
29	20	Jelen, Roman	SLO	Husqvarna	0	0	0
30	207	Seronval, Steve	BEL	Honda	0	0	0
31	7	Melotte, Cedric	BEL	Yamaha	0	0	0
32	78	Demaria, Yves	FRA	KTM	0	0	0

MX2

Overall Position	No.	Rider	Nat.	Bike	Race 1 Pos (Pts)	Race 2 Pos (Pts)	Total
1	222	Cairoli, Antonio	ITA	Yamaha	2 (22)	4 (18)	40
2	269	Vehvilainen, Jussi	FIN	Honda	6 (15)	3 (20)	35
3	15	McFarlane, Andrew	AUS	Yamaha	5 (16)	8 (13)	29
4	16	Rattray, Tyla	RSA	KTM	7 (14)	9 (12)	26
5	30	Townley, Ben	NZL	KTM	0	1 (25)	25
6	55	Nunn, Carl	GBR	Honda	11 (10)	6 (15)	25
7	4	Chiodi, Alessio	ITA	Yamaha	1 (25)	0	25
8	17	de Reuver, Marc	NED	KTM	0	2 (22)	22
9	19	Sword, Stephen	GBR	Kawasaki	16 (5)	5 (16)	21
10	90	Pourcel, Sebastien	FRA	Kawasaki	15 (6)	7 (14)	20
11	71	Maschio, Mickael	FRA	Kawasaki	3 (20)	0	20
12	76	Leok, Aigar	EST	KTM	10 (11)	14 (7)	18
13	37	Caps, Patrick	BEL	Yamaha	4 (18)	0	18
14	118	Boissiere, Anthony	FRA	Yamaha	14 (7)	11 (10)	17
15	5	Bartolini, Andrea	ITA	Yamaha	8 (13)	0	13
16	52	Leuret, Pascal	FRA	KTM	12 (9)	18 (3)	12
17	66	Stevanini, Christian	ITA	Honda	9 (12)	0	12
18	65	Monni, Manuel	ITA	Yamaha	0	10 (11)	11
19	38	van Daele, Marvin	BEL	Suzuki	20 (1)	12 (9)	10
20	711	Allier, Tomas	FRA	Kawasaki	0	13 (8)	8
21	114	Swanepoel, Garreth	RSA	KTM	18 (3)	16 (5)	8
22	22	Federici, Claudio	ITA	Yamaha	13 (8)	0	8
23	121	Salaets, Kristof	BEL	Honda	0	15 (6)	6
24	49	Goncalves, Rui	POR	Yamaha	0	17 (4)	4
25	69	Avis, Wyatt	RSA	Suzuki	17 (4)	0	4
26	377	Pourcel, Christophe	FRA	Kawasaki	0	19 (2)	2
27	68	Philippaerts, David	ITA	KTM	19 (2)	0	2
28	239	Sandouly, Frederic	FRA	Yamaha	0	20 (1)	1
29	83	Barragan, Jonathan	SPA	KTM	0	0	0
30	204	Campano, Carlos	SPA	Yamaha	0	0	0

MX1 World Championship standings:

Everts 572, Pichon 479, Coppins 441, Ramon 394, Strijbos 360, Leok 298, Jorgensen 294, Melotte 29,1 de Dijcker 211, Atsuta 181, Seguy 178, Smets 175, Burnham 175, Freibergs 157, Kovalainen 139, Gundersen 133, Noble 128, Bervoets 119, Garcia Vico 111, Theybers 111, Pyrhonen 98, Bill 85, Dobes 69, Breugelmans 56, Oddenino 50, Dini 49, Hucklebridge 47, Meo 44, Cooper 42, Martin 31, Nambotin 24, Demaria 20, Eliasson 18, Bethys 18, Flockhart 18, Jones 16, Mackenzie 11, Traversini 10, Engwall 10, Dugmore 9, Laansoo 9, Rose 8, Zerava 7, Turpin 7, Robins 5, Godrie 5, Beaudouin 4, Mossini 4, Campbell 4, Poikela 3, Izoird 3, van den Berg ,3 Kucirek 3, Nilsson 2, Das 2, Verhoeven 1, Burkhart 1, Lyons 1, Beggi 1, Lindhe 1.

MX2 World Championship standings:

Townley 497, Rattray 404, Sword 382, Cairoli 337, McFarlane 329, Chiodi 318, Maschio 303, Nunn 253, Caps 248, Federici 207, Leok 194, Boissiere 187, Pourcel 186, de Reuver 177, Dobb 154, Dement 150, Bartolini 148, Philippaerts 121, Leuret 117, van Daele 116, Barragan 109, Goncalves 105, Priem 104, Swanepoel 73, Stevanini 60, Monni 57, Vehvilainen 50, Nagl 49, Mackenzie 45, Church 41, Narita 30, Salaets 26, Avis 26, Cepelak 22, Pourcel 21, Seistola 16, Allier 12, Guarnieri 10, Cherubini 9, van Vijfeijken 8, Pirinen 7, Anderson 6, Letellier 6, Aubin 6, Smith 4, Campano 4, Barreda 3, Seronval 3, Bernardez 2, Kulhavy 2, Sandouly 1, Vromans 1.

round fourteen
Grand Prix of Europe
Gaildorf, Germany 28-29 August 2004

motocross
2004 Grand Prix Review

Yoshi Atsuta manfully holds onto the CAS Honda at Gaildorf.

round fourteen
Grand Prix of Europe
Gaildorf, Germany. 28-29 August 2004

Gaildorf is used to witnessing World Championship-winning parties. In 2001 Pichon and Dobb were crowned on the same day, while Pichon completed a successful title defence in 2002 at the venue. Ben Townley and Stefan Everts, needing only eight points over Rattray and Pichon respectively, had every chance of wrapping up their seasons with two rounds still to run, but finally were not able to don the customary celebratory t-shirts. Zolder felt far away but at the same time the season had passed in an instant. Townley was very relaxed over the weekend and his mental strength was apparent in the ways that he dismissed notions that the KTM might let him down again at a vital time or he might crack under the pressure of realising his goal. His family had flown over from New Zealand but BT seemed unperturbed about what the European Grand Prix could come to signify. During the first practice on Saturday he got involved in a fraught little scrap with Rattray (himself looking to out-psych his good friend as much as possible) and you could almost see the pair grinning at each other as they banged bars for two laps. Everts was by now well acquainted with standing on the threshold of a World Championship.

Gaildorf was another old circuit and first held a GP (250cc) twenty years earlier. There was an enormous amount of geographical space used by the club, with the riders based high in a field almost a ten-minute walk away from the paddock. Like Namur, a minibike was essential for getting around the venue. The beer tent seemed to attract half of the small town over the weekend and was the size of a football pitch. It even had a strange drink system whereby you paid for tokens and followed a line to a little hut where the pitchers of German ale were served.

Naturally, bad 1980s music was par for the course. To everyone's surprise the fast and continually cambered German circuit had a new annex consisting of a tight series of jumps and instantly added a more modern edge to the layout, even if the obstacles were not prepared that well. It had been raining hard in southern Germany leading up to the event meaning the dark mud was greasy and the paddock was also slightly swampy. Pit Beirer was visiting his home GP with other KTM dignitaries, while new German Champion Max Nagl had plenty of support and was close to running in the top ten on terrain that again was not kind

110

Rear wheels have trouble digesting green fencing. Rattray narrowly avoided this fate on Sunday.

Sebastien Pourcel looked at ease on the German jumps and accordingly scooped his first ever podium.

to the 125s in comparison to the 250s. Sword and Coppins had become British Champions over the two-week pause, while Pichon and Sebastien Pourcel were crowned in France. Gordon Crockard was making his racing return and hoping to get his speed up a notch in time for his first ever home GP two weeks later in Northern Ireland. 'Crockstar' was no longer crocked and making the last of his appearances for CAS after deciding to jump before he was pushed and signing to ride Yamahas with the Bike...It Dixon UK squad for 2005. Aprilia, who had skipped the race at Namur, were attending their last Grand Prix of the year before focussing on the supermoto version of the new bike. The World Championships had also seen the last of Brian Jorgensen. The Dane had picked up an infection in his knee during the week and wouldn't be able to compete at Gaildorf. With his condition slight and a new contract completed elsewhere Jorgensen would not race in Honda colours again in 2004.

MXTAG had a meeting with a large presence from the works teams. Only twelve squads from thirty-six had signed the YS contract, of which only four agreed with the terms. The votes collected at the meeting demonstrated a strong majority against the prize money and travel-indemnity reductions.

Significant ground was won (making the Namur press conference a slightly woolly exercise) and Youthstream allowed the teams to enter qualification in 2005 without having signed the contract (Team Suzuki were one of the strong opponents), also pledging more track advertising space for the teams as well as hosting a one-off official pre-season test in which the fee to the organisers would be given to MXTAG to split between the teams. The measures were not accepted but negotiations had begun. To what extent Youthstream were annoyed at the situation being bought to the 'table' was a matter of conjecture.

Saturday
When it came down to serious business Ben Townley was less receptive to practice hi-jinks with Rattray and kept just in front of the South African during the first qualification heat to take his tenth Saturday win of the season. Sebastien Pourcel was toying with the Kawasaki over the jumps and remained in front of de Reuver with Nagl in fifth. Former 125cc winner at Gaildorf, Mickael Maschio, was a clear winner in the second race from Federici, Chiodi and a fast Carl Nunn.

Mickael Maschio has good memories of German tracks; Gaildorf in particular. He gained his first 2004 win as teammate Sword failed to score after a heavy Saturday crash.

Maschio had earlier sustained concussion in a practice crash but was happy to joke that the prang had knocked some sense into him! Stephen Sword was also in the wars and a big fall when he caught his foot in a rut prior to dropping down into the steep gully on the fastest section of the track, required medical attention after smashing his helmet. Sword had to bail 'superman' style and hit his face in the aftermath. The British Champion was concussed and sporting a black-and-blue prizefighter complexion. Needless to say he wasn't able to take any further part at Gaildorf. The injury list was already substantial. Caps was a no-show for

the heats after straining knee ligaments in practice. Andrew McFarlane kissed goodbye to a tempestuous season when he crashed and broke his collarbone.

Mickael Pichon showed no signs of the painful memories of 2003 and immediately got on with his responsibility of showing the other MX1 riders the fastest route around the German dips and curves. The twenty-eight-year-old accordingly took his twelfth pole position of the season with a lap exactly 1.5 seconds faster than Everts. 'Tomorrow I will go for a double win,' he said later in the press conference. 'I know that Stefan has many chances to get the title but I

Keeping Everts on his toes. Mickael Pichon cured thoughts of the 2003 Gaildorf accident with an authoritative display in the second moto.

A Sunday morning warm-up crash for Carl Nunn spelled his first no-show of the season just when the Brit was looking good for a podium challenge.

will not give up and the later he wins it, the better.' Coppins, Ramon and Strijbos assumed their positions in the top five, with Enrico Oddenino setting his best qualifying time of the year on the TM in eighth.

Sunday
Carl Nunn hit the ground in a crash strikingly familiar to Sword's on Saturday, and although the Briton only had slight whiplash the medical checks took enough time to ensure that he missed both motos. The track was slippery in the morning after overnight rain. Although overcast, the showers mainly stayed away, letting the mud dry throughout the afternoon.

The MX2 motos did not go according to plan for the main protagonists. Rounding the fifth corner, a banked hairpin left, Townley ran into the back of Boissiere and went down. By the time he restarted he was last and took a further eleven laps of the twenty-one before he reached a rider to overtake. Two more circulations and he was in the pits having crashed again, and standing little chance of taking any points. It was Ben's worst race of the year and possibly at the worst time. The DNF was his sixth so far but would be his last. Rattray could only take seventh after a bad start. Maschio claimed the moto and the key result that would give him the overall victory. He was able to evade Chiodi and Federici by four seconds after an interesting battle with Cairoli had been won when the

Grand Prix of Europe

Strijbos uses all parts of his anatomy to drive the Suzuki out of the deep German ruts.

Townley is forced to watch from the pits as his title aim slips away in Germany.

Italian fell foul of the slippery mud. Pourcel was able to finish fourth with Gareth Swanepoel entering the top ten in the wake of a spicy tussle with teammate Leok.

Townley and de Reuver (who had yet more gearbox trouble in the first race) came out strongly in the second moto and the interventions of Pourcel and Cairoli made for some entertaining action. De Reuver led until the last third of the race when he lagged and Townley moved through. Attention turned to Rattray, who was riding badly further down the pack in eleventh. Townley needed his good friend to finish outside of the top fifteen if there was still a chance of the title in Gaildorf. Rattray helped slightly (and cranked up the tension) when he got on the gas exiting the first corner of the penultimate lap and the rear end lost grip, causing him to crash. He then tangled the bike up in the green fencing and was very lucky to finish the race in thirteenth without the chain spitting off the cog or the wheel locking up. Pourcel's speed in beating Cairoli to third deservedly gave him his debut World Championship podium, while Maschio crossed the line in sixth for the required points total to beat his countryman.

Pichon and Everts shared the Gaildorf MX1 motos but Pichon's turn to win arrived in the second race and therefore granted the Frenchman his thirty-third career victory. It could have been a Pichon double but the Honda man was making mistakes in the first four laps as leader in Moto1 and duly crashed. Everts

was in control, as Ramon had made a small habit of catching hay bales and was jacked out of shape on the lip of 'Sword's approach'. He pitched down the hill and was told afterwards he had a possible fracture to his right knee. Pichon quickly rallied to second place in front of Coppins and Antoine Meo, riding well on the 250cc works Kawasaki. Billy Mackenzie was holding fourth and then fifth place for half of the race before he started to also tense up and make some errors, slipping back outside the top ten. The Tiscali team made some changes to the Honda for the second race and Pichon was far less twitchy on the bike. Ramon was in pain but attempted Moto2, wishing to take points and protect his championship placing from Strijbos. The top three stayed the same from the third lap in a boring sprint. Pichon was too strong and won by almost thirty seconds from Everts, who was already thinking ahead to Ballykelly. Coppins was a country mile in front of Luigi Seguy with his best result of the season riding the Yamaha. Seguy had taken his last GP win at the circuit back in 2001. Ramon soldiered through to fifth while the ever-self-demanding Mackenzie was content with sixth, beating Strijbos by six seconds.

The corks were rescrewed in Germany and the champagne remained on ice. With two Grand Prix left to go and only 100 points remaining, the 'craic' was sure to be enjoyed for the championship leaders in Ireland.

motocross
2004 Grand Prix Review

MX1

Overall Position	No.	Rider	Nat.	Bike	Race 1 Pos (Pts)	Race 2 Pos (Pts)	Total
1	2	**Pichon, Mickael**	FRA	Honda	2 (22)	1 (25)	47
2	72	**Everts, Stefan**	BEL	Yamaha	1 (25)	2 (22)	47
3	31	**Coppins, Joshua**	NZL	Honda	3 (20)	3 (20)	40
4	24	**Strijbos, Kevin**	BEL	Suzuki	5 (16)	7 (14)	30
5	28	**Seguy, Luigi**	FRA	Yamaha	11 (10)	4 (18)	28
6	75	**Dobes, Josef**	CZE	Suzuki	7 (14)	8 (13)	27
7	211	**Mackenzie, Billy**	GBR	Yamaha	12 (9)	6 (15)	24
8	34	**Noble, James**	GBR	Honda	10 (11)	9 (12)	23
9	40	**Leok, Tanel**	EST	Suzuki	6 (15)	16 (5)	20
10	74	**Freibergs, Lauris**	LAT	Honda	13 (8)	10 (11)	19
11	43	Meo, Antoine	FRA	Kawasaki	4 (18)	0	18
12	11	Ramon, Steve	BEL	KTM	0	5 (16)	16
13	77	Kovalainen, Marko	FIN	Honda	14 (7)	13 (8)	15
14	26	Pyrhonen, Antti	FIN	TM	16 (5)	12 (9)	14
15	80	de Dijcker, Ken	BEL	Honda	8 (13)	0	13
16	18	Bervoets, Marnicq	BEL	Yamaha	9 (12)	0	12
17	27	Atsuta, Yoshitaka	JPN	Honda	0	11 (10)	10
18	21	Dini, Fabrizio	ITA	KTM	15 (6)	17 (4)	10
19	123	Oddenino, Enrico	ITA	TM	19 (2)	15 (6)	8
20	23	Crockard, Gordon	IRL	Honda	0	14 (7)	7
21	50	Hucklebridge, Mark	GBR	KTM	18 (3)	20 (1)	4
22	288	Izoird, Fabien	FRA	Suzuki	17 (4)	0	4
23	120	Dugmore, Collin	RSA	Honda	0	18 (3)	3
24	237	Boller, Andreas	GER	Honda	0	19 (2)	2
25	232	Schröter, Dennis	GER	Honda	20 (1)	0	1
26	7	Melotte, Cedric	BEL	Yamaha	0	0	0
27	261	Beconini, Manuel	ITA	Yamaha	0	0	0
28	260	Segers, David	BEL	Yamaha	0	0	0
29	48	Burnham, Christian	GBR	KTM	0	0	0
30	73	Traversini, Thomas	ITA	Aprilia	0	0	0

MX1 World Championship standings:

Everts 619, Pichon 526, Coppins 481, Ramon 410, Strijbos 390, Leok 318, Jorgensen 294, Melotte 291, de Dijcker 224, Seguy 206, Atsuta 191, Freibergs 176, Smets 175, Burnham 175, Kovalainen 154, Noble 151, Gundersen 133, Bervoets 131, Pyrhonen 112, Garcia Vico 111, Theybers 111, Dobes 96, Bill 85, Meo 62, Dini 59, Oddenino 58, Breugelmans 56, Hucklebridge 51, Cooper 42, Mackenzie 35, Martin 31, Nambotin 24, Demaria 20, Eliasson 18, Bethys 18, Flockhart 18, Jones 16, Dugmore 12, Traversini 10, Engwall 10, Laansoo 9, Rose 8, Zerava 7, Crockard 7, Izoird 7, Turpin ,7 Robins 5, Godrie 5, Mossini 4, Beaudouin 4, Campbell 4, Poikela 3, van den Berg 3, Kucirek 3, Boller 2, Nilsson 2, Das 2, Verhoeven 1, Schröter 1, Burkhart 1, Lyons 1, Lindhe 1, Beggi 1.

MX2

Overall Position	No.	Rider	Nat.	Bike	Race 1 Pos (Pts)	Race 2 Pos (Pts)	Total
1	71	**Maschio, Mickael**	FRA	Kawasaki	1 (25)	6 (15)	40
2	90	**Pourcel, Sebastien**	FRA	Kawasaki	4 (18)	3 (20)	38
3	22	**Federici, Claudio**	ITA	Yamaha	3 (20)	5 (16)	36
4	222	**Cairoli, Antonio**	ITA	Yamaha	5 (16)	4 (18)	34
5	30	**Townley, Ben**	NZL	KTM	0	1 (25)	25
6	17	**de Reuver, Marc**	NED	KTM	0	2 (22)	22
7	5	**Bartolini, Andrea**	ITA	Yamaha	13 (8)	7 (14)	22
8	76	**Leok, Aigar**	EST	KTM	9 (12)	11 (10)	22
9	16	**Rattray, Tyla**	RSA	KTM	7 (14)	13 (8)	22
10	118	**Boissiere, Anthony**	FRA	Yamaha	6 (15)	14 (7)	22
11	4	Chiodi, Alessio	ITA	Yamaha	2 (22)	0	22
12	38	van Daele, Marvin	BEL	Suzuki	10 (11)	12 (9)	20
13	49	Goncalves, Rui	POR	Yamaha	16 (5)	8 (13)	18
14	95	Nagl, Maximilian	GER	KTM	11 (10)	15 (6)	16
15	269	Vehvilainen, Jussi	FIN	Honda	19 (2)	9 (12)	14
16	114	Swanepoel, Garreth	RSA	KTM	8 (13)	20 (1)	14
17	68	Philippaerts, David	ITA	KTM	0	10 (11)	11
18	65	Monni, Manuel	ITA	Yamaha	14 (7)	18 (3)	10
19	711	Allier, Tomas	FRA	Kawasaki	12 (9)	0	9
20	52	Leuret, Pascal	FRA	KTM	18 (3)	16 (5)	8
21	66	Stevanini, Christian	ITA	Honda	15 (6)	19 (2)	8
22	377	Pourcel, Christophe	FRA	Kawasaki	0	17 (4)	4
23	121	Salaets, Kristof	BEL	Honda	17 (4)	0	4
24	251	Aubin, Nicolas	FRA	Kawasaki	20 (1)	0	1
25	253	Renet, Pierre A.	FRA	Yamaha	0	0	0
26	305	Lombrici, Robertro	ITA	Yamaha	0	0	0
27	60	Barreda, Joan	SPA	KTM	0	0	0
28	56	Priem, Manuel	BEL	Suzuki	0	0	0
29	83	Barragan, Jonathan	SPA	KTM	0	0	0
30	69	Avis, Wyatt	RSA	Suzuki	0	0	0

MX2 World Championship standings:

Townley 522, Rattray 426, Sword 382, Cairoli 371, Maschio 343, Chiodi 340, McFarlane 329, Nunn 253, Caps 248, Federici 243, Pourcel 224, Leok 216, Boissiere 209, de Reuver 199, Bartolini 170, Dobb 154, Dement 150, van Daele 136, Philippaerts 132, Leuret 125, Goncalves 123, Barragan 109, Priem 104, Swanepoel 87, Stevanini 68, Monni 67, Nagl 65, Vehvilainen 64, Mackenzie 45, Church 41, Narita 30, Salaets 30, Avis 26, Pourcel 25, Cepelak 22, Allier 21, Seistola 16, Guarnieri 10, Cherubini 9, van Vijfeijken 8, Pirinen 7, Aubin 7, Anderson 6, Letellier 6, Smith 4, Campano 4, Barreda 3, Seronval 3, Bernardez 2, Kulhavy 2, Sandouly 1, Vromans 1.

round fifteen
Grand Prix of Ireland
Ballykelly, 10-11 September 2004

Grand Prix of Ireland
Ballykelly, 10-11 September 2004

Tyla Rattray had secured runner-up position in the MX2 World Championship and was now helping a wavering Ben Townley get his kit off while dancing on top of the free bar in the Irish VIP facility. Some titles had been won in Ballykelly. Both Townley and Everts clinched their respective crowns with victory and watching the celebrations could not have provided a starker picture of two riders at the opposite end of the career scale. Everts climbed the top step for the seventh time in 2004 after winning the second moto clutching his baby son, wrapped tightly in a little Everts replica jersey. Townley had made history earlier in the day with his first 'double' since Sweden and found it just as easy to hike onto a platform later that evening and dance, while throwing his shirt to the bopping partygoers.

What might have transpired in Gaildorf occurred thirteen days later on the only Saturday Grand Prix date of the season. Ireland had not hosted a World Championship event for eight years and the Ballykelly circuit, situated just east of Londonderry, was an unknown quantity for all the riders bar Crockard and a handful of local wild cards. When the paddock arrived slightly earlier than normal the rain had already been a visitor. High winds and black clouds would retain a steady presence over the two days with Friday's activities in particular being washed out by relentless angled rainfall. The dark conditions proved a real shame for the event and the crowds were sparse in a small zone of Europe that is passionate for its motorcycle sport. The club had gone to a lot of effort in adding attractions such as a mini-moto track, 80cc support races and inviting the local BBC along to make live broadcasts from the circuit, with Everts and Townley both being interviewed at various stages in the TV rig. The track was sandy and

New British MX Open Champion Josh Coppins claims his third consecutive GP podium in a strong end-of-year flourish.

although condensed and twisty was also physically tough. The amount of water (the rain did not stop all through Friday night) turned the terrain into a bog but the wind helped drive some brighter skies across the venue on Saturday.

Friday

The Irish Grand Prix was to be Tanel Leok's last World Championship ride on the Suzuki 450 as the Motovision team had elected to crate and send the 250 to South Africa. The Estonian kept up his habit of speedy lap times in practice. He was among the top three in both 'Free' sessions, with Coppins and Pichon, and quickest in Saturday morning warm-up. Leok was just edged out to fourth in Timed Practice by Everts, who was four-hundredths of a second slower than Coppins. The slushy track cut up quickly but Pichon was revelling in the new challenge and lapped more than two seconds faster than any other rider for a customary pole. Antti Pyrhonen guided the TM to sixth behind Ramon who was in some pain from his injured leg but able to ride.

Leok is let down by the Suzuki in the Irish swamp. The Estonian came closer than ever to his maiden podium at Ballykelly.

Townley heads for a solitary walk of the track on a wet Saturday. The Kiwi had plenty on his mind with the possibility of the MX2 title only hours away.

The MX1 press conferences that evening were relaxed with Everts keeping the bigger picture in mind. 'I pushed really hard in free and qualifying sessions to do a fast lap but I failed and honestly I don't know where the problem is,' he reflected. 'We all know that it will be different tomorrow with forty-minute races, but for sure the young kids are going faster every week and sometimes I think that I'm getting old! I know that I'm close to the title, but with this bad weather everything is possible and if it won't happen tomorrow there will be two more races to go in South Africa. For sure I would prefer to secure the title here, but I'm not nervous at all.' Pichon knew the events of Saturday would probably be a formality and preferred to talk about Friday. 'Discovering a new circuit is always interesting for the riders; we've heard that there were stones and that it would be hard soil here but in fact it's a sandy track that I really like. It's technical, rough with some nice jumps. I was surprised to see the gap with my rivals, but in fact I had such a good feeling that I was really fast, especially in the second part of the track.'

The MX2 qualification heats were a KTM rout. Marc de Reuver, getting fitter and always a threat in the sand, led the first race after passing holeshotter Cairoli and also Stephen Sword, who was now on the recovery path from his virus. With his suspension set too soft Sword lost grip on the bars coming off a jump and almost crashed to hand de Reuver pole position. Townley overtook Alessio Chiodi and Patrick Caps in one lap to take second entry into the gate in the afternoon. Rattray was third ahead of Federici while Swanepoel, who by now had signed for the British Molson Kawasaki team for 2005, again looked fast. Carl Nunn was admitted to the Last Chance session after arriving less than a minute late for the cut-off time entering the waiting zone behind the start. Part jobsworth officiating and part team cock-up, the incident put another dent into the flagging morale of the RTT team, who had been running Nunn solely in the World Championships for half of the season as Jason Dougan had simply not been able to get up to speed. The Brit was third behind Maschio and Sebastien Pourcel who had crashed in the second qualification heat.

Gordon Crockard makes a pleasing comeback to action after missing the entire season. The Irishman was seventh in the second moto at his home GP.

Everts was unshakeable in his determined charge to confirm his eighth title in Ireland.

Saturday

With his seventy-ninth career victory (a new all-time record was set two years ago with his fifty-first) Stefan Everts lifted his eighth World Championship and fourth consecutive title. Ireland carried a special significance for Everts as twenty-five years ago his father Harry won the first of his 125cc Championships on the Emerald Isle. The MX1 contest gave an indelible imprint of the second half of the season. Pichon and Everts, the two best riders in the class, shared the race wins but this time it was the Belgian's turn to score the important second-moto finish.

The opening event saw a genuine contest between the two friendly foes with neither rider seeming to have the upper hand. After they had dealt with the holeshotting Melotte, Pichon led but was unable to pull away from Everts. The championship leader made a very proactive move on lap seven of nineteen when he drifted into first place. Pichon kept close and bided his time with the backmarkers coming thick and fast. The leaders lapped everybody as far as Strijbos in sixth and there was plenty of traffic on the little circuit. Pichon saw his opportunity as Everts was held up by Mackenzie and Seguy and used some more direct riding to carve a route through the groups ahead of him. He passed Everts three laps before the flag and pushed hard to open a four-second gap. Everts, once again, was less than happy with the situation and must have felt like lashing a blue flag to his handlebars for the next race, but his mood was tempered by the relief that he had finally confirmed the MX1 World Championship. Everts had his title (now winner of 125, 250, 500, MXGP and MX1 Championships) after the first moto but the party started when he passed the chequered flag for the second time. Coppins was fifty seconds away in third, in front of Melotte who had his best race since the Neeroeteren accident.

The next moto was more humdrum and Everts was able to breakaway by the time Pichon passed Coppins on the third lap. Aptly demonstrating the form that delivered his success, Everts floated around the muddy course without a care and was all the faster for it. A determination to win the Championship with an overall victory still remained and by stabilising a ten-second margin over Pichon Everts pushed his star even further into the stratosphere. Coppins was fourth behind Leok, who would have surely toasted his first overall podium if the Suzuki had not played up in the first moto.

With people surrounding the podium in a wash of congratulatory spirit, one of the well-wishers was Townley who had earlier taken delivery of his new number one plate from Steve Ramon. Like Everts, Townley had locked the title away

Party time! New MX1 World Champion Stefan Everts gives himself a champagne shower before mounting the podium with his son Liam.

Steve Ramon presents Ben Townley with the MX2 number one plate after the latter's first moto victory.

Townley crosses the finish line under a rare (and apt) moment of Irish sunshine and is mobbed.

after the first moto, but perhaps a little unlike Everts there was a fresh abundant joy of a dream being achieved for the first time.

Cairoli led off the line in Moto1 but was quickly relegated by Townley who had more than shown his capabilities in the sand this season. Just when it seemed like the nineteen-year-old would easily win the moto that gave him the championship, de Reuver popped up and began gaining on his teammate. By lap nine of eighteen the Dutchman was leading thanks to a very aggressive pass that made Townley hover on the gas. De Reuver's season would be encapsulated by lap fifteen when his bike again let him down and Townley was free to coast over the line by fifteen seconds from Rattray. Cairoli was third with Belgian Marvin Van Daele conquering the terrain to take his highest finish of the year in fourth. The factory Kawasaki's had engine problems on a very soft surface that was hard on the 4-stroke units.

A rare Townley holeshot appeared at the start of the second race (remarkably his first of the season) and he was in sensational form, pulling clear of Cairoli by almost twenty seconds before the first third of the race had passed. Leok had started in the top five and the tall Estonian produced a superb race to beat Rattray, Cairoli and de Reuver to second spot. The MX2 podium consisted of the top three riders of the 2004 season with Rattray taking third behind the new number one and the Italian. Townley's nineteenth moto win from thirty and eighth overall win of the year, not to mention the little matter of a World Championship, instigated carnival scenes from the hard-working KTM crew. Townley would take some brief time-out with his parents in the afternoon before the partying began in style at the track early that evening. KTM regained the championship they held in the class for three of the last four years. Despite the wobbles it was still an excellent advertisement for the power and application of the 250cc 4-stroke, the only full-factory prototype in the category.

A one-week break now preceded the last Grand Prix of the season and, far from ending the year on a relaxed note, the South African GP would see fireworks erupt in more ways than one.

motocross
2004 Grand Prix Review

MX1

Overall Position	No.	Rider	Nat.	Bike	Race 1 Pos (Pts)	Race 2 Pos (Pts)	Total
1	72	Everts, Stefan	BEL	Yamaha	2 (22)	1 (25)	47
2	2	Pichon, Mickael	FRA	Honda	1 (25)	2 (22)	47
3	31	Coppins, Joshua	NZL	Honda	3 (20)	4 (18)	38
4	24	Strijbos, Kevin	BEL	Suzuki	6 (15)	5 (16)	31
5	11	Ramon, Steve	BEL	KTM	5 (16)	8 (13)	29
6	7	Melotte, Cedric	BEL	Yamaha	4 (18)	13 (8)	26
7	211	Mackenzie, Billy	GBR	Yamaha	12 (9)	6 (15)	24
8	74	Freibergs, Lauris	LAT	Honda	10 (11)	9 (12)	23
9	12	Theybers, Danny	BEL	Yamaha	9 (12)	10 (11)	23
10	80	de Dijcker, Ken	BEL	Honda	7 (14)	12 (9)	23
11	40	Leok, Tanel	EST	Suzuki	0	3 (20)	20
12	77	Kovalainen, Marko	FIN	Honda	11 (10)	15 (6)	16
13	23	Crockard, Gordon	IRL	Honda	0	7 (14)	14
14	34	Noble, James	GBR	Honda	14 (7)	14 (7)	14
15	18	Bervoets, Marnicq	BEL	Yamaha	8 (13)	0	13
16	28	Seguy, Luigi	FRA	Yamaha	15 (6)	16 (5)	11
17	48	Burnham, Christian	GBR	KTM	0	11 (10)	10
18	75	Dobes, Josef	CZE	Suzuki	13 (8)	0	8
19	27	Atsuta, Yoshitaka	JPN	Honda	17 (4)	18 (3)	7
20	290	Lyons, Adam	IRL	KTM	16 (5)	19 (2)	7
21	26	Pyrhonen, Antti	FIN	TM	0	17 (4)	4
22	123	Oddenino, Enrico	ITA	TM	18 (3)	0	3
23	306	McKeown, Richard	GBR	Kawasaki	20 (1)	20 (1)	2
24	260	Segers, David	BEL	Yamaha	19 (2)	0	2
25	288	Izoird, Fabien	FRA	Suzuki	0	0	0
26	308	Sinton, Michael	GBR	Honda	0	0	0
27	43	Meo, Antoine	FRA	Kawasaki	0	0	0
28	202	Smith, Wayne	GBR	KTM	0	0	0
29	261	Beconini, Manuel	ITA	Yamaha	0	0	0

MX1 World Championship standings:

Everts 666, Pichon 573, Coppins 519, Ramon 439, Strijbos 421, Leok 338, Melotte 317, Jorgensen 294, de Dijcker 247, Seguy 217, Freibergs 199, Atsuta 198, Burnham 185, Smets 175, Kovalainen 170, Noble 165, Bervoets 144, Theybers 134, Gundersen 133, Pyrhonen 116, Garcia Vico 111, Dobes 104, Bill 85, Meo 62, Oddenino 61, Mackenzie 59, Dini 59, Breugelmans 56, Hucklebridge 51, Cooper 42, Martin 31, Nambotin 24, Crockard 21, Demaria 20, Eliasson 18, Bethys 18, Flockhart 18, Jones 16, Dugmore 12, Traversini 10, Engwall 10, Laansoo 9, Rose 8, Lyons 8, Zerava 7, Izoird 7, Turpin 7, Robins 5, Godrie 5, Beaudouin 4, Mossini 4, Campbell 4, Poikela 3, van den Berg 3, Kucirek 3, Boller 2, Segers 2, Nilsson 2, Das 2, McKeown 2, Verhoeven 1, Schröter 1, Burkhart 1, Lindhe 1, Beggi 1.

MX2

Overall Position	No.	Rider	Nat.	Bike	Race 1 Pos (Pts)	Race 2 Pos (Pts)	Total
1	30	Townley, Ben	NZL	KTM	1 (25)	1 (25)	50
2	222	Cairoli, Antonio	ITA	Yamaha	3 (20)	4 (18)	38
3	16	Rattray, Tyla	RSA	KTM	2 (22)	5 (16)	38
4	76	Leok, Aigar	EST	KTM	8 (13)	2 (22)	35
5	114	Swanepoel, Garreth	RSA	KTM	13 (8)	6 (15)	23
6	49	Goncalves, Rui	POR	Yamaha	5 (16)	14 (7)	23
7	55	Nunn, Carl	GBR	Honda	10 (11)	10 (11)	22
8	4	Chiodi, Alessio	ITA	Yamaha	7 (14)	13 (8)	22
9	83	Barragan, Jonathan	SPA	KTM	12 (9)	9 (12)	21
10	17	de Reuver, Marc	NED	KTM	0	3 (20)	20
11	118	Boissiere, Anthony	FRA	Yamaha	16 (5)	7 (14)	19
12	68	Philippaerts, David	ITA	KTM	11 (10)	12 (9)	19
13	38	van Daele, Marvin	BEL	Suzuki	4 (18)	0	18
14	37	Caps, Patrick	BEL	Yamaha	15 (6)	11 (10)	16
15	269	Vehvilainen, Jussi	FIN	Honda	6 (15)	0	15
16	22	Federici, Claudio	ITA	Yamaha	0	8 (13)	13
17	90	Pourcel, Sebastien	FRA	Kawasaki	9 (12)	0	12
18	56	Priem, Manuel	BEL	Suzuki	14 (7)	0	7
19	69	Avis, Wyatt	RSA	Suzuki	0	15 (6)	6
20	65	Monni, Manuel	ITA	Yamaha	0	16 (5)	5
21	121	Salaets, Kristof	BEL	Honda	0	17 (4)	4
22	226	de Belder, Tom	BEL	Honda	20 (1)	18 (3)	4
23	249	Bradshaw, Neville	RSA	Suzuki	18 (3)	20 (1)	4
24	60	Barreda, Joan	SPA	KTM	17 (4)	0	4
25	711	Allier, Tomas	FRA	Kawasaki	0	19 (2)	2
26	242	Anderson, Brad	GBR	KTM	19 (2)	0	2
27	19	Sword, Stephen	GBR	Kawasaki	0	0	0
28	5	Bartolini, Andrea	ITA	Yamaha	0	0	0
29	426	Lewis, Gregory	GBR	Suzuki	0	0	0
30	71	Maschio, Mickael	FRA	Kawasaki	0	0	0
31	52	Leuret, Pascal	FRA	KTM	0	0	0

MX2 World Championship standings:

Townley 572, Rattray 464, Cairoli 409, Sword 382, Chiodi 362, Maschio 343, McFarlane 329, Nunn 275, Caps 264, Federici 256, Leok 251, Pourcel 236, Boissiere 228, de Reuver 219, Bartolini 170, Dobb 154, van Daele 154, Philippaerts 151, Dement 150, Goncalves 146, Barragan 130, Leuret 125, Priem 111, Swanepoel 110, Vehvilainen 79, Monni 72, Stevanini 68, Nagl 65, Mackenzie 45, Church 41, Salaets 34, Avis 32, Narita 30, Pourcel 25, Allier 23, Cepelak 22, Seistola 16, Guarnieri 10, Cherubini 9, van Vijfeijken 8, Anderson 8, Pirinen 7, Aubin 7, Barreda 7, Letellier 6, Bradshaw 4, de Belder 4, Smith 4, Campano 4, Seronval 3, Bernardez 2, Kulhavy 2, Vromans 1, Sandouly 1,

Grand Prix of South Africa

Sun City, 25-26 September 2004

motocross

Grand Prix of South Africa
Sun City, 25-26 September 2004

Mickael Pichon won his sixth Grand Prix of the season, Greg Albertyn made an emotional farewell in front of his fans and Ben Townley chalked off victory number nine in his championship campaign. The South African Grand Prix however – the first flyaway event for four seasons – will be remembered for two other incidents. The first MX1 moto was delayed by ten minutes after the riders agreed to stage a brief strike in protest at Youthstream's payment cuts. The officials were dumbstruck as Everts, Pichon, Coppins and co. refused to budge from the waiting zone and the live TV coverage was accordingly affected. Youthstream and FIM bosses hurried down from the VIP facilities to see what was going on but exactly ten minutes after the race was supposed to commence the riders kick-started and filtered through onto the line. The circuit commentator announced that there had been some 'technical trouble'; there was more trouble to come. Everts, as World Champion and a senior figure, said in a private conversation after the moto that the protest was merely the 'first' until Youthstream agreed to listen to the riders. Sadly, any good work achieved by the new MX1 number one in representing and supporting the views of his fellow professionals was erased within a minute of the second race. Adhering to the timetable on this occasion the pack steamed around the first lap. Yoshi Atsuta surprisingly took the holeshot but eyes were quickly diverted a few positions further back. Everts scaled a small right-turn jump on the outside of the track while Pichon threw the Honda up the inside and got on the gas exiting the rise. His line pulled him across the circuit into the path of Everts. The Honda touched the Yamaha's front wheel and pitched the Belgian onto the ground. Jumping up holding his shoulder, everybody watched amazed as

Top: A moment of madness. Everts invades the track to confront an approaching Pichon.
Bottom: Saturday afternoon winds covered the paddock in dust, played havoc with the track structures and saw the MX2 heats cancelled.

Everts climbed over the track wall and ran to the adjacent corner where the riders were coming back around. Pichon was up to third but had to avoid an incensed World Champion who had invaded the track and went to throw his goggles at the Frenchman. It wasn't over yet. Everts remounted and toddled around the circuit. Albertyn was leading by now from Pichon and the group came up to lap the blue and red Yamaha. Watching the fast-approaching gaggle over his shoulder Everts manoeuvred the 450 onto the inside line of the tight chicane around the back of the circuit to deliberately block Pichon, almost causing him to crash.

The behaviour was so out of the ordinary it was actually hard to believe. Everts pitted at the end of the lap and stormed out of the circuit, forgetting to attend the podium ceremony and collect his number-one plate, which furthered angered the series' promoters. It was a controversial and sensational way to finish the year. After apparently organising a defiant gesture earlier in the day (despite the fact that a whole gate of riders refused to leave the pens, not just Everts) Youthstream and the FIM now knew that they had the perfect ammunition with which to fire the book at the World Champion. The Belgian, who has been a courteous and professional ambassador of the sport for so many years, immediately knew he had done wrong. 'Pichon made a really aggressive move on me that I also thought was really dangerous, and I was so furious with him that as he came around for the next lap I threw my goggles at him. I know this was wrong and I should not have reacted like I did. Unfortunately it happened and I cannot turn back time. I have been to the jury meeting and I made an apology for what I did.' 'The second moto did not really go as I would have expected!' said eventual winner Pichon afterwards. 'It started well except for that little incident I had with Stefan. He was aggressive in the first lap, like he has been many times this year, and I understand this because he wants to win, like I do. I came to the inside and he went far outside and to the middle, I had already jumped out in the middle also and we touched and I took his front wheel. I know it was perhaps not a nice move but he did the same to me last year in Austria and I was lucky to stay on the bike. I just wanted to make the move and there was nothing else involved. Afterwards his reaction was not so nice, he was probably very mad and again I can understand this because I would have been the same! He tried to push me on the corner by the finish line and when he was on the bike again the next lap he almost put me on the ground and I nearly crashed. This might not be a good end to the Championship but I just wanted to win really badly.'

There were rumours within a few hours that Everts would face a ban and maybe miss the start of next season. Youthstream also confirmed, in the run-up

Everts was seen as the organiser of the MX1 riders' strike. His misdemeanour later in the day ruined any chance of being a spokesman for his peers in the future.

to the Motocross of Nations the following weekend, that they would seek some retribution and were considering a large fine upon the teams for their riders' actions; a move that hardly would have been ideal for the current rifts in the paddock. There was a large lobby of support for Everts, especially from Townley who stated that if the World Championship saw fit to ban their top rider then he would be better off out of it and leave for America.

At the Nations six days later Everts and Pichon held a joint press conference to clear up the dispute. Each reading statements (Everts apologising, Pichon accepting) they then shook hands and the matter was over. The FIM passed the case onto the international disciplinary court in November and dragged Everts and Pichon to Geneva, where they imposed a 10,000 euro fine between them and Everts received a suspended ban for two years. This effectively severed his powers as a future political agent or spokesman for his peers. The ruling was especially harsh considering the largely democratic nature of the protest.

Despite being rivals for most of the season and since they first squared-up in 2003, Pichon and Everts have maintained a good relationship based on a lot

of respect for the other's achievements. Pichon has stated on more than one occasion that beating Everts meant defeating the top motocrosser ever, while Everts has never regarded Pichon as anything but a complete equal. In the absence of Smets, the pair were also united in a common goal to air the riders' protests against Youthstream's legislation.

Sun City was frankly an amazing place to end 2004. The holiday resort crosses a boundary between luxurious haven and a theme park. Many people arrived a few days earlier or left a little later to enjoy the wild nature reserves nearby, the crocodile sanctuary, the water sports park or simply marvel at one of the most amazing hotels in the world, The Palace. From its location on top of the hill surveying the resort, a series of smaller lower-class hotels offered a more affordable means of accommodation. It was all an illusion of course. Often referred to as 'man-made oasis', Sun City had to be reached by a two-hour drive from Johannesburg through some shanty towns that offered a totally contrasting perspective.

The fact that the contents of the paddock were all located together in the same hotel (the cheapest) was very appropriate and forged a nice sense of community. The motocross travelling village had truly become so. Not everyone could afford to make the expenses of the trip. The MX1 and MX2 entries were the smallest of the season and half of the field for the MX2 motos were local riders. Sun City had paid a lot of hard cash to host a Grand Prix and it showed. Courtesy buses ferried people around and the circuit was a mammoth project beginning with the ground up. Built on a section of the car park near the entrance of the resort, a very supercross feeling was fashioned by transporting the stadium sections, normally reserved for exclusive golfing events, and enclosing three sides of the facility with seating for up to 17,000 fans. A decent PA, a paddock using the asphalt of the car park (no mud at this GP), good TV camera positions and five-star hospitality gave the venue a very professional sheen. There were drawbacks. The two marquees erected to form paddock garages with flimsy dividers were too small and the whole thing shook violently during Saturday's blustery conditions. The teams were operating out of crates but more attention could have been paid to their needs and comfort; the VIPs were much better off. The stadium seating ensured great views of the action, but like the MotoGP circuit in Valencia there is a lofty level of detachment being so far away from the bikes; any atmosphere was hard to contain. The crowds did not turn up in the expected figures touted beforehand by the organisers and the one-third-full stands on Sunday uncovered a glaring piece of misinformation/propaganda by the club and Youthstream

Above: James Noble completed a quiet and problematic World Championship campaign with a good showing in Sun City.
Opposite: Townley and Sword share air time in one of the most exciting battles of 2004.

when the official figure declared was a double-visioned 21,000. Seven or eight thousand would have been a nearer estimate.

The track had an adventurous layout but any plaudits won by the course were lost by the terrain, which was like rock. The essential element of the Grand Prix did not measure up to the rest of the circuit's high standards. A deep, sandy straight section flanked by two corners offered a reminder of St Jean. One nice touch was the effort put into making the event a memorable sporting occasion. A small opening ceremony was held with dancers in local costumes bearing flags and letting off fireworks. It was a token gesture but was a reminder that an international annual competition was being staged; European promoters would do well to try and create motocross as more of a 'show'. The weather over the weekend was great with plenty of sun. Saturday presented a few problems when some strong winds appeared in the afternoon and started blowing advertising hoardings around, making the paddock tent wheeze. The gusts were so problematic that the MX2 heats were scrapped in favour of a half-hour qualification session.

Former double-250cc World Champion Greg Albertyn had stopped riding full time in 2001, mainly due to injury. The first Grand Prix in his country for nineteen years was a perfect opportunity to sign off a successful career. He asked for, and warmly received, help from Team Suzuki (with whom he won his last title in 1994) and became the second rider in 2004 to use Smets' machinery. There was little doubt that 'Albee', now a real estate agent, was the star of the event, even if Tyla Rattray was also clocking up a fair amount of time in front of the cameras. On Friday evening the Suzuki rider was awarded the prestigious Lifetime Achievement award by the South African Department of Sport. He would go on to be surprisingly fast during practice after 'burning the candle at both ends for the past five weeks' and his motos were like night and day. Multiple crashes and a retirement in the opening race were quickly erased when he led the world for the first two laps of the second and crossed the line in a very worthy sixth, sending the fans home happy. For Andrea Bartolini and Marnicq Bervoets it was not only the last GP of the season but also of their long careers. Bervoets had not had a happy year at all and would probably prefer to tell people that he retired at the end of 2003 in years to come. It had not been a fulfilling campaign for Bartolini either, but such is the high regard in which he is held, a special award was presented to the Italian on Sunday night.

Saturday

Everts was hunting his eightieth career victory. As a great believer in little coincidences, an eightieth win to fall in the same season as the eighth world title would be motivation enough to give Sun City his best shot. In the second free practice he was within a hundredth of a second of Pichon's fastest time after the Frenchman had originally set the pace from Greg Albertyn in the morning session. The South African would twist his ankle in the second period but was still able to qualify ninth after the chrono on his first-ever day riding a

'Albee' was back for one last shot and instigated the biggest cheer of the day when he led the second moto for two laps.

450 4-stroke. Pichon wasn't about to release his welded grip on MX1 Timed Practice. He was virtually a second-and-a-half faster than Everts with Coppins in third and Strijbos fourth. RWJ Honda rider James Noble was up to sixth and both TMs were top-ten fixtures.

The wind was howling at times and covering the loosely constructed paddock in dust and debris. The pit lane was an unbearable place to be unless you

Grand Prix of South Africa

de Reuver finally rested with the New Zealander taking Pole. Five riders were within half a second and it was an interesting sign for Sunday.

Sunday

The first MX1 moto was a demonstration of speed by Mickael Pichon who left Everts, Coppins and Strijbos behind in the first two laps. Everts could do nothing about the escaping Honda but knew very well from Ireland that the second race would be the key to the 'overall'. Pichon won his tenth moto of the season with a massive forty-second gap back to Coppins in third. Albertyn had struck a fallen Bervoets going through the sand for the first time and was ramped by Atsuta who was making his last appearance as a Honda rider. Two more small crashes led to a painful retirement for Albee. Billy Mackenzie reached as high as sixth behind Ramon and Strijbos after passing factory Yamaha rider Melotte. Ramon made sure of fourth place in the championship with his ride, and the vastly different second moto would give him another podium to round off his first season in the series.

The exhilarating early moments of the second moto prompted an interesting last race of the 2004 season. Everts' retirement was incredibly the first DNF for the Yamaha rider in three years and gave Pichon a clear track to head for only his second double-GP win. Albertyn's crowd-rousing lead lasted two laps before Pichon got the better of him and began to separate from the small group. On lap eight the championship runner-up got out of shape in the sand pit and crashed, falling five positions down the order as he fished the Honda out of the sand and back on the track. Coppins now ran the show as Pichon began to charge back, all the while over the large jumps looking around to see how much ground he had to make up to his Honda compatriot. Pichon had to at least overtake Ramon in second spot if he wanted the overall win and managed to shut down a considerable time deficit to pass the Belgian without hassle four laps from the finish. Coppins had his second moto victory of the year after maintaining a strong pace but Pichon's hard work to capture second allowed his sixth win of the season.

Aigar Leok had won the Belgian Championship at the end of August and was finishing the MX2 season on a shiny note. The Estonian's rise from eighteenth on the first lap to third position during Moto1 was the highlight of the day. As the last regular in the pack (in front of eleven wild cards) he cut past fourteen riders in eighteen laps before pouncing on Swanepoel just before the chequered flag. It was a powerful performance and fittingly gave the teenager his first top three. Swanepoel was disappointed not to hold onto third spot but his fourth place was also a career best. A close second to Leok's blitzfor entertainment factor was the

Cairoli keeps an eye on the pursuing World Champion.

borrowed a rider's goggles to see what was going on. Ben Townley was almost blown clean off the track while jumping the large finish-line table top, and that was the catalyst for the heats to be cancelled for an MX1 style qualification process. Although the action of the Saturday races had gone, the chrono still provided some exciting moments. Swanepoel and Rattray headed the timing screens entering the last minute before a blur of changes involving Pourcel, Townley and

Andrea Bartolini signs off his career with a champagne dousing.

fight for the lead in the same race. Stephen Sword had recently been rejected and then reinstated into the British Motocross of Nations teams in the farce that was the selection procedure for the 2004 competition. Feeling healthier and burning with the frustration of losing third place in the championship (as well as the indignity of the Nations snub) Sword was out to leave his mark on what had still been the best season of his career. The Kawasaki rider took the race directly to Townley and Rattray and the threesome circulated closely for almost half the distance, level hitting the jumps and trying different lines to gain an advantage. Townley was having to work to defend his lead more than at any stage during the year. Sword was up to the task of winning motos once more and Rattray was riding pumped for his home race. By lap nine, just as Sword had taken the lead, it came to an end. The Kawasaki's gearbox failed and he registered his ninth moto DNF in nine Grand Prix. Rattray harried the World Champion as much as he could but number 30 was not to be budged from the top of the lap chart. BT had the track 'nailed'. The KTM rider's timing on the jumps was pinpoint-accurate every lap and this made the difference over the scurrying desperation of Rattray, who was changing his lines to find some extra speed.

Townley's twenty-first and final moto victory arrived later in the hot afternoon and this time Cairoli was the aggressor. The race was not as frantic as the first but Cairoli did not let Townley escape and had to watch over his own shoulder as Rattray was not relinquishing the chase. The Italian collected a fifth podium result in a marvellous breakthrough season and rested third in the standings. Pourcel was fourth after triumphing in a private scrap with Patrick Caps. Sword had less influence after a few tepid opening laps limited him to sixth place.

The season had ended and the riders and paddock removed the official team clothing for the last time to gather together at the dinner/awards ceremony taking place in one of the main exhibition halls on the complex. The large number of tables accommodated several hundred people with local delicacies being tucked into as much as the free bar. There was an atmosphere of relief hovering over, with murmurings as the championship had at last finished, but there was also an uneasiness directly related to the afternoon's episode and the ripples it would cause. This intensified in a stilted prize-giving ceremony. Cairoli bounced up to collect an ugly-looking rookie of the year award but Everts was more subdued picking up his medal, while FIM delegates were even more serious. Everts jokingly mentioned in a very short speech that he hoped he might be able to 'ride next season' but any thin traces of humour evaporated with the wall of stern faces around him on the stage. A further bad-taste effect was generated

Coppins spectacularly charts the progress of a chasing Mickael Pichon. The Honda rider would score his second moto victory of the year in Sun City.

when Sun City were given the 'Best GP of the year award' in front of British and Swedish representatives and the Africans celebrated in overblown fashion. The organisation had been excellent but was certainly not faultless and if truth be known there were better rounds in terms of the track and the atmosphere.

Finally the food was laid out and the party began. The sight of riders drinking and stuffing their faces like mere mortals was an eye-opener. Some of the dancing later in the resort's disco was also a precious moment. 2004 had been wrapped-up, and what a journey it had been.

133

MX1

Overall Position	No.	Rider	Nat.	Bike	Race 1 Pos (Pts)	Race 2 Pos (Pts)	Total
1	2	Pichon, Mickael	FRA	Honda	1 (25)	2 (22)	47
2	31	Coppins, Joshua	NZL	Honda	3 (20)	1 (25)	45
3	11	Ramon, Steve	BEL	KTM	5 (16)	3 (20)	36
4	24	Strijbos, Kevin	BEL	Suzuki	4 (18)	4 (18)	36
5	7	Melotte, Cedric	BEL	Yamaha	7 (14)	7 (14)	28
6	27	Atsuta, Yoshitaka	JPN	Honda	11 (10)	5 (16)	26
7	34	Noble, James	GBR	Honda	8 (13)	10 (11)	24
8	72	Everts, Stefan	BEL	Yamaha	2 (22)	0	22
9	77	Kovalainen, Marko	FIN	Honda	14 (7)	8 (13)	20
10	75	Dobes, Josef	CZE	Suzuki	15 (6)	9 (12)	18
11	26	Pyrhonen, Antti	FIN	TM	12 (9)	12 (9)	18
12	40	Leok, Tanel	EST	Suzuki	10 (11)	14 (7)	18
13	511	Albertijn, Greg	RSA	Suzuki	0	6 (15)	15
14	48	Burnham, Christian	GBR	KTM	16 (5)	11 (10)	15
15	211	Mackenzie, Billy	GBR	Yamaha	6 (15)	0	15
16	80	de Dijcker, Ken	BEL	Honda	9 (12)	0	12
17	288	Izoird, Fabien	FRA	Suzuki	17 (4)	15 (6)	10
18	123	Oddenino, Enrico	ITA	TM	20 (1)	13 (8)	9
19	120	Dugmore, Collin	RSA	Honda	13 (8)	0	8
20	202	Smith, Wayne	GBR	KTM	19 (2)	16 (5)	7
21	330	Fourie, Freddie	RSA	KTM	18 (3)	18 (3)	6
22	710	Venske, Craig	RSA	Suzuki	0	17 (4)	4
23	331	Van der Berg, Dewald	RSA	Yamaha	0	19 (2)	2
24	338	Fitz-Gerald, Darryl	RSA	KTM	0	20 (1)	1
25	336	Hanekom, Hentie	RSA	Honda	0	0	0
26	337	Davies, Shane	RSA	Yamaha	0	0	0
27	18	Bervoets, Marnicq	BEL	Yamaha	0	0	0

MX1 World Championship standings:

Everts 688, Pichon 620, Coppins 564, Ramon 475, Strijbos 457, Leok 356, Melotte 345, Jorgensen 294, de Dijcker 259, Atsuta 224, Seguy 217, Burnham 200, Freibergs 199, Kovalainen 190, Noble 189, Smets 175, Bervoets 144, Pyrhonen 134, Theybers 134, Gundersen 133, Dobes 122, Garcia Vico 111, Bill 85, Mackenzie 74, Oddenino 70, Meo 62, Dini 59, Breugelmans 56, Hucklebridge 51, Cooper 42, Martin 31, Nambotin 24, Crockard 21, Demaria 20, Dugmore 20, Eliasson 18, Bethys 18, Flockhart 18, Izoird 17, Jones 16, Albertijn 15, Traversini 10, Engwall 10, Laansoo 9, Rose 8, Lyons 8, Zerava 7, Smith 7, Turpin 7, Fourie 6, Robins 5, Godrie 5, Beaudouin 4, Venske 4, Mossini 4, Campbell 4, Poikela 3, van den Berg 3, Kucirek 3, Boller 2, Van der Berg 2, Nilsson 2, Segers 2, Das 2, McKeown 2, Verhoeven 1, Fitz-Gerald 1, Schröter ,1 Burkhart 1, Lindhe 1, Beggi 1.

MX2

Overall Position	No.	Rider	Nat.	Bike	Race 1 Pos (Pts)	Race 2 Pos (Pts)	Total
1	30	Townley, Ben	NZL	KTM	1 (25)	1 (25)	50
2	16	Rattray, Tyla	RSA	KTM	2 (22)	3 (20)	42
3	222	Cairoli, Antonio	ITA	Yamaha	5 (16)	2 (22)	38
4	76	Leok, Aigar	EST	KTM	3 (20)	7 (14)	34
5	37	Caps, Patrick	BEL	Yamaha	6 (15)	5 (16)	31
6	90	Pourcel, Sebastien	FRA	Kawasaki	12 (9)	4 (18)	27
7	22	Federici, Claudio	ITA	Yamaha	7 (14)	10 (11)	25
8	114	Swanepoel, Garreth	RSA	KTM	4 (18)	15 (6)	24
9	118	Boissiere, Anthony	FRA	Yamaha	11 (10)	8 (13)	23
10	55	Nunn, Carl	GBR	Honda	10 (11)	9 (12)	23
11	4	Chiodi, Alessio	ITA	Yamaha	8 (13)	11 (10)	23
12	5	Bartolini, Andrea	ITA	Yamaha	9 (12)	13 (8)	20
13	49	Goncalves, Rui	POR	Yamaha	14 (7)	12 (9)	16
14	19	Sword, Stephen	GBR	Kawasaki	0	6 (15)	15
15	69	Avis, Wyatt	RSA	Suzuki	15 (6)	14 (7)	13
16	332	de Jager, Jarret	RSA	Yamaha	13 (8)	16 (5)	13
17	334	Fitz-Gerald, Kerim	RSA	KTM	17 (4)	18 (3)	7
18	245	Simpson, Shaun	GBR	KTM	16 (5)	19 (2)	7
19	325	Sandiford-Smith, Oliver	GBR	KTM	0	17 (4)	4
20	322	Stegen, Karl	RSA	Honda	18 (3)	0	3
21	320	Branch, Ross	RSA	Honda	19 (2)	0	2
22	344	van der Westhuizen, R	RSA	Yamaha	0	20 (1)	1
23	336	Peterson, Leonard	RSA	Yamaha	20 (1)	0	1
24	335	Ford, Shaun	RSA	Honda	0	0	0
25	342	Terreblanche, Shannon	RSA	Yamaha	0	0	0
26	321	Brito, Brett	RSA	Yamaha	0	0	0
27	323	Bircher, Brett	RSA	Yamaha	0	0	0
28	333	Topliss, Ian	RSA	Suzuki	0	0	0
29	345	Kruger, Shaun	RSA	Yamaha	0	0	0
30	17	de Reuver, Marc	NED	KTM	0	0	0
31	324	Sternagel, Uwe	NAM	Yamaha	0	0	0
32	71	Maschio, Mickael	FRA	Kawasaki	0	0	0

MX2 World Championship standings:

Townley 622, Rattray 506, Cairoli 447, Sword 397, Chiodi 385, Maschio 343, McFarlane 329, Nunn 298, Caps 295, Leok 285, Federici 281, Pourcel 263, Boissiere 251, de Reuver 219, Bartolini 190, Goncalves 162, Dobb 154, van Daele 154, Philippaerts 151, Dement 150, Swanepoel 134, Barragan 130, Leuret 125, Priem 111, Vehvilainen 79, Monni 72, Stevanini 68, Nagl 65, Mackenzie 45, Avis 45, Church 41, Salaets 34, Narita 30, Pourcel 25, Allier 23, Cepelak 22, Seistola 16, de Jager 13, Guarnieri 10, Cherubini 9, van Vijfeijken 8, Anderson 8, Pirinen 7, Simpson 7, Aubin 7, Fitz-Gerald 7, Barreda 7, Letellier 6, Sandiford-Smith 4, Smith 4, Bradshaw 4, de Belder 4, Campano 4, Stegen 3, Seronval 3, Bernardez 2, Branch 2, Kulhavy 2, Peterson 1, Vromans 1, Sandouly 1, van der Westhuizen 1.

2005

The 2005 FIM Motocross World Championships faces an uneven political path but the calendar, originally showing seventeen races with two visits to the UK and another flyaway to Japan, showed signs that Youthstream's ambitions were getting bigger and better and they were trying to stay true to their promises. Whether there is a concrete base on which to build for the future remains unchecked, even though there were plenty of observers offering opinions both for and against.

MX1 will see some new faces, as well as the same individuals but in different colours. Townley completes a three-pronged KTM effort while Jorgensen will be Yamaha-bound. Javier Garcia Vico was saved from the wilderness by Tiscali Martin Honda and now rides shotgun to Pichon. Smets will be back for perhaps one last season while Strijbos also committed short-term to MX1. Leok will steer the new Kawasaki 4-stroke and Everts will undoubtedly see number 9 and be thinking of a perfect 10.

MX2 has Rattray and de Reuver on the championship-winning bikes as Melotte, Cairoli and Chiodi will be Yamaha's best hopes. Kawasaki will be looking at Sword and Pourcel to mount a challenge for regular GP wins, as Honda considerably bolster their lineup by bringing in 2001 AMA 125cc champion Mike Brown to partner Erik Eggens at RWJ. Promising riders such as Aigar Leok, Gareth Swanepoel, Christophe Pourcel and Max Nagl will have more backing and be eager to repeat the success-laden path that Cairoli walked in 2004. The wheels turn and the trophies will again be polished for another season.

Fox Motocross of Nations
Lierop, Holland, 2-3 October 2004

Fox Motocross of Nations
Lierop, Holland, 2-3 October 2004

Some serious issues clouded the build-up to the fifty-eighth edition of the prestigious Motocross of Nations at Lierop. For the third time in four years Team USA were not going to be travelling to Europe. The competition always had a 'Ryder Cup' edge to it with the American Motocross series being so strong, and the AMA's decision not to send a team was disappointing. The federation cited budget concerns and the fact that the tournament wasn't aired on TV, nor attracted any interest back in the United States. Their claims were made to look quite ridiculous by the presence of countries like Canada, Japan, Guatemala, Australia, New Zealand and Russia, and also by the public declarations of riders like Travis Pastrana to support a USA entry. Ricky Carmichael had recently switched from Honda to Suzuki and issued an honest open letter to the press stating that he could not give his best at a time when he did not know the bike and team. Having been a staunch supporter of the MoN, and part of the team that finished runners-up to Belgium in 2003, Carmichael's concern was understood and accepted. Excuses from other parties ranged from injury concerns to a dislike of the sand. In the end the Americans were not represented but the Nations turned out to be a real festival of motocross in spite of the absence of some of the sport's big names; it was a case of who really missed whom?

Several other American-based stars dipped out. Tortelli and Vuilleman turned down the opportunity to represent France while Australian Chad Reed could have returned to the track where he scored his GP win in an international rookie season in 2001. The close proximity of the race to the cash-pot that is the US Open could have been a factor in a seemingly widespread boycott.

Top: Battle scars. Everts reveals the wounds of a training accident that could easily be representative of the battering his name had taken since South Africa.
Bottom: Billy Mackenzie earned his MX1 placing in a controversially decided Team GB but Sunday's races were not a positive experience for the Scot.

137

motocross
2004 Grand Prix Review

Stefan Everts and the repercussions of the South African incidents were the talk of the paddock and had a wealth of commentary. To paint him even more the 'villain' in the eyes of the authorities he had crashed while practicing during the week and had broken his cheekbone, leaving his face and eye a bit of a mess.

After several different selections and widespread derision Team Great Britain arrived with a three-man squad. Whether it was the correct team, or even the strongest one, had the British fans and industry in endless debates in the weeks and days preceding the races. Paul Cooper's inclusion after six months out of GPs was certainly contentious. A damp effort to ninth overall was dogged by bad luck but the critics weren't satisfied. The success story of the Nations was not only Belgium's fourteenth triumph or Holland's first podium result since 1991, but also in the event itself. The atmosphere was a real cosmopolitan carnival of colours and international banter. A figure of 30,000 people for the event was definitely nearer the mark than South Africa. The bands of support around the packed sandy setting of Lierop were noisy and appreciative. The racing was half-decent despite the clear advantage the Belgians and Dutchmen held in the terrain (deeper than Valkenswaard and Lichtenvoorde), and the circuit – as usual with the Mac Club – was excellent with a challenging track, big-screen television, impressive hospitality and a wide, open (and flat!) paddock.

Above left: Giuseppe Luongo and FIM's Wolfgang Srb undergo a press conference grilling in Lierop.
Above: Everts forgot about the off-track distractions and produced a first-class performance for Belgium.

Sunday

Off the track, two press calls were essential viewing. In front of the biggest press attendance of the year (over 150 journalists and photographers) a battered Everts apologised to Pichon while still calling his move 'very dangerous' in a prepared statement, Pichon accepted and said 'I hope whatever is decided by the disciplinary commission keeps the general interest of Motocross in mind,' in support of his rival. Then the FIM and Youthstream gave a bizarre press conference in which they announced little and left themselves open for a Q+A in which they were criticised for the lack of harmony in the paddock and their perceived inaction in healing the divisions. The validity of their information provision was called into question in the wake of the South African audience-data fabrication. The questions/accusations seemed to be taken personally and were by no means satisfactorily answered. The whole affair was tense but at least some accountability was being demanded from the controllers of the sport; worryingly nothing surfaced. The accessibility to Youthstream and the FIM is a positive factor on their part but maybe there is too much talking and at a politically very sensitive time a more low-key profile would have maintained their image, instead of the publicity damage that the Sunday press conference caused. After having some time to reflect on the incident Giuseppe Luongo duly returned at the end of the day to shake Everts' and Pichon's hands at the post-podium conference and announce that Youthstream would not be pursing the riders or teams for financial retribution from the South African strike; engineered or not it was a gesture that gave a pleasant end to the international season.

The Nations had returned to the old format of three races, three classes and three riders per team. The three motos mixed two categories so everybody raced against each other and the five best results accumulated by each team (a reverse points-scoring system) at the end of the day were totalled and the lowest tally produced the champions. The MX1 class had Everts against the likes of de Reuver (riding a 250cc 2-stroke), Coppins, Tanel Leok, Vehvilainen, Crockard and Paul Cooper. MX2 saw Townley facing Rattray, Sword, Cairoli, Ramon, Eggens and Akira Narita. Lastly the MX Open category was mainly a shoot-out between Pichon and Strijbos.

The stars of the races on a cloudy but temperate day were Everts for Belgium along with de Reuver and Erik Eggens for Holland. Putting aside the distraction of a temporarily distorted face (that would be fixed by surgery the week after) and rumours of a large impending penalty, Everts was able to defeat a fired-up and inspired de Reuver in both motos with deadly precision. The track became very rough after Saturday's qualification heats (in which seven of the twenty-seven nations were not able to make the cut) and the long split-rhythm section adjacent to the pits was crumbling; the fastest route becoming a swift weave between the jumps.

In the first race between MX1 and MX2, Everts capitalised on a de Reuver mistake five laps before the flag to win. Erik Eggens, having been out for the entire season, had lost twenty kilos and trained for months to be ready, was riding

Strijbos hears the grunt of the Honda and knows that Pichon is closing in.

a 125cc 2-stroke but could finish eleventh to place the Dutch second behind early leaders New Zealand (Coppins was third and Townley sixth). The Kiwis' chances of victory exploded, along with Townley's KTM, halfway through the next moto. The TV image of the World Champion engulfed by a giant plume of smoke from the deceased engine as he rolled to a halt midway through the race was grandiose. Pichon easily defeated Strijbos and an impressive Juss Laansoo (Estonia) in the second moto with Ramon's improved seventh position on the KTM 250 moving Belgium into the lead for the first time. Great Britain suffered with Stephen Sword being knocked out in the first moto after being hit by Cairoli. The Briton could barely ride in the next race and retired. Paul Cooper's steady if unspectacular finishes of eleventh and twelfth helped the team stay in the top ten.

Everts had to be on his toes to fend off first Pichon and then de Reuver in the last event. Strijbos' sixth position was enough to ensure the Suzuki rider's first Nations team victory in his debut appearance. Belgium were champions for the second year in succession. De Reuver's runner-up spot was cheered all the way by the fans and guaranteed a popular second position. Dutch Open Champion Bas Verhoeven was the third member of the team. The chase for the final step of the podium was incredibly tight. France, Estonia and South Africa finished level on

points, and France eventually grabbed the trophy because their sixth and worst result was the better of the trio. Sebastien Pourcel's seventeenth in the first race had the advantage over Laansoo's nineteenth in the final moto and Wyatt Avis's twenty-ninth in the same sprint. Tanel Leok's exhaust broke and he was passed by Coppins for fourth on the final lap of the first race. The moment of misfortune lost the Estonians an historic top-three finish.

Party time for the Belgians was also a crowning moment on a momentous season for Everts. His performance at the Nations as leader of a young team also reinforced what a precious jewel the World Champion is to motocross.

Left: Two in a row for Belgium as Holland celebrate a popular home podium.
Below: Erik Eggens (59) was back and in some style. The Dutchman's efforts on the 125 earned him a high-ranking Honda ride for 2005.

Moto1 Classification (MX1+MX2):

Position	No.	Rider	Nat.	Bike	Difference
1	1	Everts, Stefan	BEL	Yamaha	00:00.0
2	58	de Reuver, Marc	NED	KTM	00:22.2
3	10	Coppins, Joshua	NZL	Honda	00:42.7
4	7	Vehvilainen, Jussi	FIN	Honda	00:47.3
5	22	Leok, Tanel	EST	Suzuki	01:11.9
6	11	Townley, Ben	NZL	KTM	01:27.1
7	32	Rattray, Tyla	RSA	KTM	01:28.4
8	19	Crockard, Gordon	IRL	Honda	01:32.5
9	25	Meo, Antoine	FRA	Kawasaki	01:46.8
10	31	Swanepoel, Gareth	RSA	KTM	01:56.1
11	59	Eggens, Erik	NED	KTM	02:00.2
12	71	Barragan, Jonathan	SPA	KTM	02:10.5
13	2	Ramon, Steve	BEL	KTM	02:12.6
14	67	Goncalves, Rui	POR	Yamaha	1 lap
15	13	Mackenzie, Billy	GBR	Yamaha	1 lap
16	23	Leok, Aigar	EST	KTM	1 lap
17	26	Pourcel, Sebastien	FRA	Kawasaki	1 lap
18	50	Cairoli, Antonio	ITA	Yamaha	1 lap
19	37	Eliasson, Joakim	SWE	Honda	1 lap
20	8	Seistola, Matti	FIN	Honda	1 lap

Moto2 Classification (MX2+Open):

Position	No.	Rider	Nat.	Bike	Difference
1	27	Pichon, Mickael	FRA	Honda	00:00.0
2	3	Strijbos, Kevin	BEL	Suzuki	00:36.0
3	24	Laansoo, Juss	EST	Honda	00:54.1
4	32	Rattray, Tyla	RSA	KTM	01:16.9
5	9	Pyrhonen, Antti	FIN	TM	01:23.2
6	78	Blair, Morgan	CAN	Yamaha	01:30.6
7	2	Ramon, Steve	BEL	KTM	01:35.5
8	60	Verhoeven, Bas	NED	Honda	01:51.0
9	59	Eggens, Erik	NED	KTM	01:55.3
10	18	Atsuta, Yoshitaka	JPN	Honda	01:59.8
11	15	Cooper, Paul	GBR	Honda	02:01.9
12	23	Leok, Aigar	EST	KTM	02:04.8
13	42	Boyd, Shane	AUS	KTM	02:14.7
14	26	Pourcel, Sebastien	FRA	Kawasaki	02:16.2
15	12	Hurley, Daryl	NZL	Suzuki	1 lap
16	33	Avis, Wyatt	RSA	Suzuki	1 lap
17	71	Barragan, Jonathan	SPA	KTM	1 lap
18	30	Kadlecek, Michal	CZE	Yamaha	1 lap
19	57	Schröter, Dennis	GER	Honda	1 lap
20	56	Schiffer, Marcus	GER	Yamaha	1 lap

Moto2 Classification (MX2+Open):

Position	No.	Rider	Nat.	Bike	Difference
1	1	Everts, Stefan	BEL	Yamaha	00:00.0
2	58	de Reuver, Marc	NED	KTM	00:03.8
3	27	Pichon, Mickael	FRA	Honda	00:14.7
4	31	Swanepoel, Gareth	RSA	KTM	00:45.1
5	22	Leok, Tanel	EST	Suzuki	00:46.5
6	3	Strijbos, Kevin	BEL	Suzuki	01:12.3
7	67	Goncalves, Rui	POR	Yamaha	01:31.0
8	7	Vehvilainen, Jussi	FIN	Honda	01:38.7
9	9	Pyrhonen, Antti	FIN	TM	01:46.3
10	13	Mackenzie, Billy	GBR	Yamaha	01:56.2
11	19	Crockard, Gordon	IRL	Honda	02:03.8
12	15	Cooper, Paul	GBR	Honda	02:06.0
13	76	Roy, Jean Sebastien	CAN	Honda	02:08.2
14	25	Meo, Antoine	FRA	Kawasaki	02:08.9
15	60	Verhoeven, Bas	NED	Honda	1 lap
16	78	Blair, Morgan	CAN	Yamaha	1 lap
17	12	Hurley, Daryl	NZL	Suzuki	1 lap
18	42	Boyd, Shane	AUS	KTM	1 lap
19	24	Laansoo, Juss	EST	Honda	1 lap
20	55	Nagl, Maximilian	GER	KTM	1 lap

Overall Standing:

1.	Belgium	17
2.	Netherlands	32
3.	France	41
4.	Estonia	41
5.	Republic of SouthAfrica	41
6.	Finland	46
7.	New Zealand	76
8.	Canada	79
9.	Great Britain	86
10.	Portugal	90

motocross
2004 Grand Prix Review

Overall Results

MX1:

Pos.	Rider	FLA	SPA	POR	NED	GER	BEN	GBR	FRA	ITA	BEL	SWE	CZE	WAL	EUR	IRL	RSA	Total
1	Everts, Stefan	32	50	47	47	42	50	38	50	47	40	40	44	45	47	47	22	688
2	Pichon, Mickael	30	14	47	36	23	33	47	22	42	47	45	50	43	47	47	47	620
3	Coppins, Joshua	36	42	20	16	33	30	47	42	35	36	20	40	44	40	38	45	564
4	Ramon, Steve	43	26	33	27	33	22	29	34	34	36	33	24	20	16	29	36	475
5	Strijbos, Kevin	20	20	28	31	13	38	18	8	43	36	40	32	33	30	31	36	457
6	Leok, Tanel	23	22	12	17	21	26	32	26	21	28	14	31	25	20	20	18	356
7	Melotte, Cedric	47	22	34	47	38	42	20	18	23	0	–	–	0	0	26	28	345
8	Jorgensen, B.	25	22	13	–	50	–	13	25	21	35	42	32	16	–	–	–	294
9	de Dijcker, Ken	7	22	16	27	12	11	27	4	22	12	14	21	16	13	23	12	259
10	Atsuta, Y.	8	6	23	20	10	14	9	22	16	1	16	12	24	10	7	26	224
11	Seguy, Luigi	–	–	–	7	14	–	22	29	27	28	10	29	12	28	11		217
12	Burnham, C.	8	6	13	12	10	24	10	22	18	16	6	22	8	0	10	15	200
13	Freibergs, L.	–	18	11	18	5	23	0	19	13	18	10	10	12	19	23		199
14	Kovalainen, M.	11	0	6	13	1	16	12	14	6	12	24	8	16	15	16	20	190
15	Noble, James	21	14	12	–	–	9	20	14	2	12	5	8	11	23	14	24	189
16	Smets, Joel	22	30	10	40	36	16	21	–	–	–	–	–	–	–	–	–	175
17	Bervoets, M.	13	13	6	11	28	0	26	0	–	–	–	9	13	12	13	0	144
18	Pyrhonen, A.	8	8	15	9	7	13	–	–	–		24	5	9	14	4	18	134
19	Theybers, Danny	13	2	9	16	16	18	–	–	–	10	7	6	14	–	23		134
20	Gundersen, K.	28	33	32	27	13	–	0	–	–	–	–	–	–	–	–	–	133
21	Dobes, Josef	2	0	6	0	–	–	–	15	15	7	3		21	27	8	18	122
22	Garcia Vico, F.	10	32	23	0	19	27	–	–	0	–	–	–	–	–	–	–	111
23	Bill, J.	–	–	–	–	–	–	–	12	24	18	–	16	15	–	–	–	85
24	Mackenzie, B.	–	–	–	–	–	–	–	–	–	–	–	–	11	24	24	15	74
25	Oddenino, E.	0	0	0	0	0	4	11	6	7	3	14	2	3	8	3	9	70
26	Meo, Antoine	0	4	0	0	–	4	7	14	8	–	–	5	2	18	0		62
27	Dini, Fabrizio	1	2	–	–	–	–	–	8	2	8	15	–	13	10	–	–	59
28	Breugelmans, S.	7	–	–	–	–	0	–	0	–	20	12	12	5	–	–	–	56
29	Hucklebridge, M.	6	8	1	9	1	0	0	–	–	8	14	–	–	4	–	–	51
30	Cooper, Paul	15	13	14	–	–	–	–	–	–	–	–	–	–	–	–	–	42

MX1 Manufacturers:

Pos.	Team	FLA	SPA	POR	NED	GER	BEN	GBR	FRA	ITA	BEL	SWE	CZE	WAL	EUR	IRL	RSA	Total
1	Yamaha	25	25	22	25	22	25	20	25	25	22	20	22	25	22	25	16	366
2	Honda	20	22	25	18	25	18	25	22	20	25	25	25	22	25	22	25	364
3	Suzuki	13	16	15	20	18	20	18	16	22	16	18	18	18	18	18	18	282
4	KTM	22	20	18	15	15	13	16	20	16	20	16	13	13	9	16	20	262
5	TM	0	0	0	0	0	2	5	0	3	0	14	0	1	7	0	10	42
6	Kawasaki	0	0	0	0	0	0	1	5	4	0	0	0	0	10	0	0	20
7	Husqvarna	–	–	–	–	–	–	–	–	–	0	0	0	0	0	0	0	0
8	Aprilia	–	–	–	–	–	–	–	–	0	0	0	0	0	0	0	0	0

MX2

Pos.	Rider	FLA	SPA	POR	NED	GER	BEN	GBR	FRA	ITA	BEL	SWE	CZE	WAL	EUR	IRL	RSA	Total
1	Townley, Ben	47	25	47	50	25	50	50	25	33	25	50	45	25	25	50	50	622
2	Rattray, Tyla	15	42	26	44	25	44	44	37	14	40	19	28	26	22	38	42	506
3	Cairoli, A.	6	22	27	31	28	40	–	33	34	14	22	40	40	34	38	38	447
4	Sword, Stephen	38	36	45	33	45	31	40	20	18	0	36	19	21	–	0	15	397
5	Chiodi, Alessio	–	–	21	34	16	29	21	36	35	17	44	40	25	22	22	23	385
6	Maschio, M.	26	31	10	13	44	0	31	36	18	38	14	22	20	40	0	0	343
7	McFarlane, A.	36	37	25	30	22	29	30	1	50	25	15	–	29	–	–	–	329
8	Nunn, Carl	15	13	28	28	7	22	29	19	17	13	17	20	25	–	22	23	298
9	Caps, Patrick	–	2	0	5	33	36	20	23	31	31	33	16	18	–	16	31	295
10	Leok, Aigar	31	30	14	5	13	18	16	21	5	14	4	5	18	22	35	34	285
11	Federici, C.	13	–	–	27	38	1	11	36	36	0	14	23	8	36	13	25	281
12	Pourcel, S.	5	18	16	8	15	0	9	17	23	35	0	20	20	38	12	27	263
13	Boissiere, A.	16	12	10	–	11	–	23	28	17	12	19	22	17	22	19	23	251
14	de Reuver, Marc	43	18	42	18	0	–	–	–	–	–	–	34	22	22	20	0	219
15	Bartolini, A.	–	9	15	17	0	–	5	0	23	0	38	28	13	22	0	20	190
16	Goncalves, Rui	16	0	0	9	0	9	6	8	8	15	16	14	4	18	23	16	162
17	Dobb, James	27	22	22	7	27	15	22	0	–	12	–	–	–	–	–	–	154
18	van Daele, M.	1	23	12	0	11	9	6	4	17	22	1	0	10	20	18		154
19	Philippaerts, D.	14	13	16	18	–	13	9	18	2	9	7	0	2	11	19		151
20	Dement, Jeff	7	3	8	12	20	15	–	–	23	38	24	0	–	–	–	–	150
21	Swanepoel, G.	–	9	2	13	5	10	3	–	1	1	8	13	8	14	23	24	134
22	Barragan, J.	15	19	1	11	12	20	0	9	0	7	–	15	0	0	21		130
23	Leuret, Pascal	13	0	19	–	19	–	7	9	14	0	19	5	12	8	0		125
24	Priem, Manuel	21	7	14	–	0	9	5	19	0	16	13	–	–	0	7		111
25	Vehvilainen, J.	–	–	–	–	–	–	–	–	–	–	–	15	35	14	15		79
26	Monni, Manuel	12	1	3	–	–	2	0	4	6	8	7	3	11	10	5		72
27	Stevanini, C.	–	–	7	–	–	10	4	7	4	16	0	0	12	8	–	–	68
28	Nagl, M.	0	–	–	3	10	–	0	16	4	13	–	3	–	16	–	–	65
29	Mackenzie, B.	8	–	11	14	0	–	11	1	–	–	–	–	–	–	–	–	45
30	Avis, Wyatt	–	5	–	–	3	–	0	–	0	–	14	0	4	0	6	13	45

MX2 Manufacturers:

Pos.	Team	FLA	SPA	POR	NED	GER	BEN	GBR	FRA	ITA	BEL	SWE	CZE	WAL	EUR	IRL	RSA	Total
1	KTM	25	25	25	25	14	25	25	25	16	25	25	25	18	16	25	25	364
2	Yamaha	18	22	16	20	20	20	15	20	25	16	22	22	25	20	22	20	323
3	Kawasaki	20	20	22	18	25	16	20	22	14	22	18	13	12	25	4	15	286
4	Honda	15	11	18	14	15	13	16	10	13	20	15	10	22	6	14	11	223
5	Suzuki	13	14	7	0	4	4	3	9	8	13	6	0	2	9	8	6	106

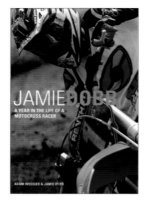

JAMIE DOBB
A SEASON IN THE LIFE OF MOTOCROSS WORLD CHAMPION
Adam Wheeler & Jamie Dobb

Jamie Dobb is the country's most successful Motocross racer of recent times after becoming Britain's first ever 125cc World Champion at the age of twenty-nine. This action-packed book recounts the twists and turns of his 2002 250cc World Championship campaign as a factory rider with KTM. Offering a fascinating glimpse into the life of a Motocross World champion with all that it entails – fear, crashes, broken bones, excitement, training and gritty determination – this book is an essential read for any Motocross fan.

0 7524 2880 2

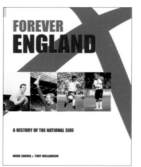

FOREVER ENGLAND
A HISTORY OF THE ENGLAND SIDE
Mark Shaoul & Tony Williamson

From the days of amateur gentlemen of the 1870s to the present day, Forever England is an insightful and fascinating account of the history of the country's national football team. England's finest hour in 1966 is covered in detail, as are the other highs and lows of 130 years of international competition. This enthralling narrative includes England team line-ups for key games, match reports and every group table involving England from all major tournaments, and is richly illustrated with over 200 images.

0 7524 3202 8

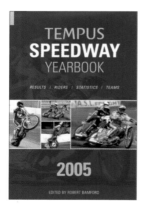

TEMPUS SPEEDWAY YEARBOOK 2005
Robert Bamford

As part of their ongoing association with the sport of speedway, Tempus are proud to be producing the second edition of their national speedway annual. This volume will appeal to all followers of the shale sport – both old and new. Containing all the results, teams and riders from the 2004 season, with colour action shots and personality profiles from an unforgettable campaign, this is a publication that no speedway fan should be without.

0 7524 3396 2

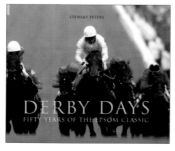

DERBY DAYS
FIFTY YEARS OF THE EPSOM CLASSIC
Stewart Peters

Since it was first run in 1780, the Epsom Derby has become one of the great events in the sporting calendar. The most prestigious and important flat race event of the year, it attracts crowds in excess of 50,000 every year from all walks of life. This book covers the runners and riders of the last fifty years, with a dramatic retelling of all the major action and many excellent photographs.

0 7524 3202 8

If you are interested in purchasing other books published by Tempus, or in case you have difficulty finding any Tempus books in your local bookshop, you can also place orders directly through our website
www.tempus-publishing.com